Canny Leek Growing

Canny Leek Growing

by Daniel A. Calderbank

British Library Cataloguing in Publication Data

Calderbank, Daniel A.
    Canny leek growing.
    1. Leeks—Great Britain
    I. Title
    635'.26   SB 351.L5

    ISBN 0-946707-03-0

First published in November 1984 by
RightAngle Books, an imprint of
Intercept Limited, P.O. Box 402, Wimborne,
Dorset BH22 9TZ, England

Reprinted October 1987

Filmset in Plantin by
Photo-Graphics, Honiton, Devon
Printed by A. Wheaton and Company
Limited, Marsh Barton, Exeter, Devon

TO CAROL

Contents

Illustrations

The cover illustration shows the author with his pot leek 'Elliot's Original'. The following illustrations will be found between pages 52 and 53:

Introduction

The leek, with origins in the Middle East, is one of the oldest of cultivated vegetables; it has had both culinary and herbal uses. For well over a century the leek has also been a popular exhibitor's vegetable in some selected areas of Britain.

The pot leek in particular has close links with the North Eastern mining community where, for a time, it was known as the pitman's leek – this may have been an unfortunate stigma which perhaps inhibited its acceptance in other parts of the country. The Royal Horticultural Society included it in their Horticultural Show Handbook only as recently as 1981!

The pot leek is an integral part of the social life in the areas where it is popularly grown. Raising the pot leek demands a full twelve months' preparation and cultivation, thus providing the leek grower with a full-time interest. There is much rivalry in this male-dominated pastime.

The subject of pot leeks is synonymous with the North East of England. Each former mining village had its own show and if the village had more than one public house there would invariably be two (or more!) leek shows. In the cities of Durham and Newcastle upon Tyne scores of leek shows were, and are, held each year throughout September and into October.

Although it was the men alone who raised the plants for exhibition, the show itself became a family concern. In the early years the room was decorated for the occasion and the show lasted throughout a weekend, sometimes including Monday and Tuesday as well. The prizes were often items for the home, and during the show and the following week a leek broth was served freely to all who attended the hostelry. The leeks for the broth would be of relatively poor quality, such as would never attain the show-bench; some shows still provide a 'leek supper'.

The use of leeks for the 'pot' may have given rise to the naming of these short, stocky plants. A second derivation is one that compares the leeks to a 'pot of ale' which would be in a vessel some six inches high and of large diameter — a model for all pot leek growers.

Friendly competition and a common subject for conversation could be had by raising leeks, without any fear of losing the manly status associated with a miner. Despite increased local populations, the demise of many coalfields,

1

and the advent of other forms of leisure, the pot leek remains closely enmeshed with the social life of the North East. Everything else may have changed but pot leeks provide a link between past and present; growing pot leeks is, to many, a Religion.

Leek plants (and the 'know-how' of growing them) are handed down through families. There are some leek trenches that have been cultivated for generations: when a leek grower has to move home it is not unknown for bags of soil to be removed as well as furniture. Conversations at work, in the allotments, and in the public house never reveal the whole truth. The leek grower will hold back some vital piece of information in order to maintain a dominance on the showbench.

In fact, information is sometimes designed to be misleading; for example, the apparent necessity to feed the leeks on steeped sheep manure (collected early in the morning with the dew still evident) has had many growers who are anxious to improve their leeks, searching the moors and common lands. The administration of large quantities of beer filtered through the kidneys and applied to the leeks after closing time, has more devotees, particularly if the allotment is on the way home from the pub!

My knowledge of horticulture helped me to dispel the myths of leek growing and (being a native of Lancashire) I had no pre-conceived ideas about how to grow them. I listened, asked questions and learned; I had soil analysed; I experimented with various leek strains, and ultimately I became knowledgeable.

This book withholds no information: leek growing and exhibiting is a hard enough pursuit without having the misfortune to be lacking in knowledge. However, there are so many variations in the cultivation of the leek that there is scope for experimentation. Indeed, some strains of leek require modifications to the standard pattern of cultivation. Finally, new fertilizers and plant hormones are available to be tried, making leek growing an area of potential constant improvement. ... Good growing!

SECTION ONE

This section examines the history of leeks from their earliest beginnings. It includes the social importance of pot leeks in specific areas of Britain and explains how the pot leek has become an increasingly popular exhibition vegetable.

1

The History of Leeks in General

The origin of the leek (*Allium porrum*) has been lost in antiquity, but there is little doubt that it developed from the wild leek (*Allium ampeloprasum*) which, although it is to be found in Britain, remains rare. The leek grower, however, would have little difficulty in recognizing the wild plant because it has many similarities to today's leek, including the strap-like leaves, pale purple to whitish flowers with a few small bulbils, and a papery brack, or sheath, protecting the head before the flowers open.

The very close relatives of the leek include the onion, chives and garlic; more distant relatives include all members of the lily family.

The origin of the cultivated leek appears to have been in one of the Eastern Mediterranean countries where it has been grown since prehistoric times. While the leek today is grown for showing and for culinary purposes, its original use was medicinal as well as culinary.

The Bible mentions the leek, in particular in the account of the Exodus in Numbers, chapter 11, verse 5. The Israelites state that they 'remember the fish, which we did eat in Egypt freely; the cucumbers, and the melons, and the leeks, and the onions and the garlick'. The Exodus is thought to be about 1500 BC with the leek being a popular food in Egypt at the time of the Pharaohs. It is one of our oldest, if not *the* oldest, cultivated vegetable.

The Romans were possibly introduced to the leek by the Egyptians, but it was their Emperor, Nero, who gave it some notoriety. Once a month, Nero went on a 'leeks-in-oil' diet, giving up all other food, in order to lubricate his throat and clear his voice. The less respectful called him 'Porrophagus' though no doubt only among themselves!

It is my belief that the Romans introduced the leek to Britain during their occupation between AD 43 and AD 410. They certainly introduced onions, cabbage, lettuce, parsnips and many herbs — ensuring a healthier diet than that of the native population.

William Aiton, a gardener for King George III, stated in his book *Hortus Kewensis* that leeks were brought to England in 1562. However, Tusser refers to leeks in his *Hundred Pointes of Good Husbandrie*, published as early as 1557. Alexander Nickham (1157–1217), the Abbot of Cirencester, included leeks in a list of vegetables and herbs that every garden should contain. The word 'leek' gives some indication of its history, for the term *leac tun* is Anglo-Saxon for 'leek enclosure'. Today we might use the term kitchen garden or allotment.

Speculation surrounds the connection between the Welsh and the leek. White and green, the colours of the leek, are the Cymric colours, and it is suggested that the leek has been the emblem of Wales since the time of St David, and commemorates a victory over the Saxons. The Welsh soldiers wore the leek in their hats so that they could distinguish between themselves and the enemy more clearly. How tragic it would have been to have lost one's hat and been bludgeoned to death by a fellow Welshman! The wearing of the leek is likely to be much more recent, aided and abetted by Shakespeare.

The leek is a useful winter vegetable, particularly when there is little else growing, and the fact that it is hardy and needs no storage must have increased its popularity in the North. Here the winter months are long and a vegetable with a season from autumn to spring must have been welcome.

W. Robinson in his book *The Vegetable Garden*, first published in 1885 reports that 'the fine qualities of this vegetable are much better known to the Welsh, Scotch and French than to the English or Irish'. He also mentions the large quantities of leeks being grown in the valley of the Thames where the soil is moist. These must have been for markets elsewhere, for he goes on to mention that in the south of England the value of the vegetable is little known except to good cooks.

To a cook, one leek must look the same as any other, but there are many varieties of *Allium porrum* reported. In the early years of this century there were over ten varieties; since the Common Market regulations were introduced the numbers available through seed merchants have declined.

Leeks that were available many years ago included the 'Long Paris Winter Leek', a hardy variety with a natural long blanch area. 'Long Mezières Leek' was hardy, but thicker, while the 'Bulgarian Leek' was tender and used only as a summer leek. The 'London Flag Leek' was also tender, as was the 'Large Yellow Poitou Leek' originating in the west of France. The 'Large Rouen Leek' was slow to run to seed, giving a long harvesting season, and the 'Giant Carentan Leek' was an improvement, being larger in size. 'Flanders Winter Leek' was very frost hardy but had a tendency to produce suckers — a problem not uncommon today with some exhibitors' leeks. The 'Perpetual Leek' was a curiosity, producing many shoots; the 'Brabant Short Broad

Leek' was small but hardy, while the 'Lion Leek' (syn. 'Lyon'?) was the most popularly grown in England.

The 'Musselburgh' or 'Scotch Flag Leek' is the most famous one, deriving its name from the town near Edinburgh. The broad leaves, greater length and thicker portions made this leek popular, and it is still available today.

The short stout 'stemmed' varieties developed in the North of England and South Scotland are known as pot leeks and are equally numerous. The geography of their origins is certain, but exactly when these leeks were developed is less certain.

2

Leeks in the North East of England

The leek has held a very high position in the north of England and in Scotland and perhaps more in North East England than elsewhere. Prior to 1974 this area included Northumberland (the area north of the river Tyne) and County Durham to the south of the Tyne. Today this area is classified as Northumberland, Tyne and Wear and County Durham.

The extent to which this vegetable has held such high esteem, is evident in the naming of the shows. Many were described as a 'leek, flower and vegetable show', i.e. leeks came first! The leek was, and still is, supreme; but what kind of leeks were they, how was the judging carried out, and are comparisons possible?

Gardening magazines such as those we are familiar with today could have provided the information. Unfortunately, the few magazines that existed then, concentrated upon the sort of gardening familiar only to the gentry. Information on peaches and nectarines, vines and figs is readily available, but the working classes of the north with their leeks, pigeons and ferrets might just as well not have existed!

However, local newspapers had to concern themselves with parochial interests, and shows were certainly visited by their reporters. Regrettably (as with newspaper reports today) the objective of the reporter is to establish who the winners are. Occasionally the prizes are mentioned, but rarely any information is given on the judging, or on the number and type of leeks exhibited.

At present, leeks are judged according to their length of blanch — there are long, intermediate and pot leeks. However, there is some confusion about the length at which a pot leek becomes an intermediate, and an intermediate becomes a long leek. Add to this the variation in judging, i.e. whether it is inclusive of cubic capacity or otherwise (according to tradition, it is;

9

however, according to the Royal Horticultural Society it is not). The RHS, incidentally, have only recently (1981) recognized the pot leek as a show vegetable and do not include the intermediate leek at all in their Horticultural Show Handbook. If this kind of confusion exists today, then trying to analyse the events of around 100 years ago is likely to meet with little success.

In 1863 for example, at the Durham Floral and Horticultural Society Show two shillings (equivalent to 10 p) was the first prize for the best six leeks. In 1875, at the Lumley and Harraton Flower Show three leeks comprised a stand, whereas in 1883, at the Ferryhill Flower Show, four leeks were required 'with their tops left on'! Although it may seem improbable to us now, apparently at some shows the leeks were exhibited only after decapitation.

The size of leeks holds a great interest to all exhibitors, but comparisons are largely invalid. Not until the introduction of my computer-accurate measurement tables and a standard measuring tool have leeks been measured accurately. Even using these, the size of leeks can vary considerably, depending where on the leek the judge places the measuring tape. The pair of leeks exhibited as recently as 1979 by Alan Herbert, and at 194.3 cubic inches heralded as a record, was open to doubt while still on the showbench!

A chapter in this book is devoted to judging, but I hope the reader is now able to view past show reports with some reservations. For example, in 1904, at the New Inn, Washington, the Coronation Leek Club is reported to have held its annual show in the first floor rooms. The judge, John Winters, measured the prize-winners at 112 cubic inches. The prizewinner, J. Self, received a pair of blankets; W. Storey in second place a dinner set, and W. Curry, in third position, a china tea set. A pair of leeks at 112 cubic inches is very commendable (the pair of leeks winning the first Pot Leek Society Show in 1978 measured 111.9 cubic inches). However, the report on the 1904 show fails to mention the number of leeks; it was probably three but could have been more, making the leeks rather less impressive by today's standards. Sizes can be compared only when the number of leeks exhibited is known; even then, the way in which they are measured may give rise to great inaccuracies.

Prizes awarded at leek shows invariably included household items and this tradition still exists in many of the leek shows held in the North East. An arrangement is usually made with a large department store, where all the goods for the show will be purchased. The prize offered can either be accepted, or an alternative of the same value chosen from the store.

In this comparatively affluent society household goods are perhaps less desirable than they were half a century or more ago. Just why this tradition started is another puzzle, but it at least ensured that the home benefited from the horticultural activities of the husband, rather than any prizemoney being spent on the other interests of the husband!

In 1883 'a superb display of leeks was exhibited at the Gilligate Giant's Annual Vegetable Show'. First prize was five shillings (25 p), second three shillings (15 p) and third a bottle of spirit! Other prizes at this show included a shoulder of mutton, a heart and tongue and two neck ties.

In 1893, 16 members of the 'Pot and Glass' Leek Club at Crossgate Moor all received a prize in this, their seventh annual show. First prize was a pair of blankets and a picture. Club shows today share the funds accumulated over the year between all the members entering the show. Naturally, the division of the fund is unequal, depending upon whether one is first, last, or somewhere in between — but herein lies the incentive to do well and to raise the leeks to the best of one's ability.

At Leadgate, in the same year, the sixth annual open leek show was held, attracting 27 entries. An open show is one which anyone can enter and, in this respect, differs from a 'members only' show. Open shows are usually sponsored by a local business and are often the best because they attract many of the top exhibitors. In a 'members only' show, entrants may have one good leek grower to contend with, but an open show may have top leek growers from the whole of the North-East area in contention.

The Durham City Annual Show (established 1880) and regarded (at least in 1893) as the premier show of the North, had 440 entrants for the vegetable classes, but there was only a small display of leeks. Three leeks comprised a stand and these measured 16 inches, 15 inches and 12½ inches long with the circumferences ranging from 5½ to 6 inches. If these had been exhibited today they would have covered two categories — long and intermediate! There was, however, no mention of measurement in cubic inches, in the published report.

Local newspaper reporters were kept busy throughout September and early October reporting on all the shows, describing them as 'Local Flower Shows' or 'Leek Club Shows'; nevertheless, even under the former name it was the leek results that dominated. As mentioned previously, the reporting left a lot to be desired and some accounts were very brief indeed: for example, at Willington on 31 August 1895, it is recorded that 'prizes for best leeks were awarded to W. Cox and R. Harris' — no other information was given!

Some shows gained a little more coverage, perhaps to fill a particular page, or (more than likely) the reporter was given more hospitality at the venue of the show, which was often a local hostelry. At the Travellers's Rest, Framwellgate Moor, it was reported in 1895 that 30 people exhibited at this first annual leek show, which was promoted by the working men of Framwellgate Moor and Pity Me. Three leeks comprised a stand and the prizewinners were G. Dobinson, J. Baker, and T. Dobinson. Each exhibitor received a 'useful article' as a prize but these are not specified and there are no other details. There is little more that one can glean from this report, other than it was a good show, with 90 leeks on show, and that the Dobinson family must have been less well liked at the end of the day than on the day previous — such is the price of success!

Quite often a special prize was offered for the best leeks in the show, usually the best single leek. An exhibitor who had raised one exceptional leek, but who failed to gain a first prize because of the poor quality of his other leeks in the stand, thus might gain the special prize. Members of the Middle Herrington and District Leek Club in 1895 held their show at the house of Mr Joseph Allinson, Board Inn, Herrington, with awards totalling over £12. In addition, a prize of a silver medal was available for the best leeks.

Most of the club shows were held at public houses and the landlord sometimes received mention, as above, if not the hostelry itself. For example, a show was held at Mr Lumsden's hostelry at Crossgate in 1895, where three leeks comprised a stand. W. Golightly took first place and a prize of £1 15s (£1.75p); W. Robson, second, (£1 and a sheep's heart), and T. Stewart, third, 15 shillings (75 p) and 'a beast's heart'. A special prize was awarded to Mr Robson for the best single leek in the show.

The New Seaham Inn leek club held their show in 1895 at the inn which was then in the hands of Mr B. Murray. The report states that there was a very large and commendable display of leeks and other vegetables in the 'long room', which was 'very neatly decorated'. T. Curry, J. Brown and J. Parker were the prizewinners for the leeks. The report concludes that valuable prizes were offered by the committee and 'everyone was satisfied with the awards'.

Decorating the room in which the leeks were exhibited was common practice. Although it probably was not necessary at the general shows where other vegetables and flowers would add colour, it is likely to have been prevalent at the leek shows; and I am tempted to think that this arose from the desire of the women folk to become involved and to make the show 'pretty'. To a leek exhibitor a leek show is a spectacle in itself and needs no dressing, but to the ladies the leeks must have resembled rows of cadavers on a mortuary slab.

One novel way of getting the show decorated was to offer prizes for the floral decorations. In 1895 the Durham Flower Show was held in the Town Hall and New Markets. Special prizes were awarded for the decoration of the fireplaces in the drawing room. Three leeks comprised a stand; Mr N. Walker of Gateshead won first prize, and Mr Lawson of Sunderland came second. Two of the three winning leeks were mentioned: these measured 11 inches by 6 inches and 10¼ inches by 6¼ inches. Following the pattern of other shows at this time, the first figure would be the length and the second the circumference. Such leeks today would be classed as intermediate.

Other shows where mention is made of the decorations include one at Auton Stile at the Dog and Gun Inn in 1895. The room was 'gaily decorated' and exhibits and prizes were well arranged on the tables. From the 21 entries, the first three prizewinners were J. Cooke (blankets and quilt); J. Blake (blankets and cornice pole), and J. Curran (blankets and spade).

In the same year, at the Salutation Inn, Framwellgate Moor, the report mentions the 'tasteful decoration of the room with flowers, plants and other adornments'. Unfortunately, the leeks were far from first-rate quality, although each exhibit did secure a useful prize. The first three were M. Hutchinson (chest of drawers and looking glass); Mr. Straffair (swing rocking chair), and Mrs. Straffair (swing lamp).

It must be admitted that leek growing and exhibiting is very much a male-dominated affair: women exhibitors are seen as either 'comedians' or (what is more likely) they are thought to provide scope for their husbands to enter another pair of leeks and gain another prize at the show! Whether the Straffair family were, in fact, thus resented by other members is not known.

Decorating the room by the landlord of the hostelry also appears to be commonplace. In 1907 the Silksworth Colliery leek club held their show at the Vane Arms Hotel, Silksworth and Mr and Mrs C. Binding, host and hostess, 'tastefully decorated the room'. In addition, the centre of the room displayed 'a large assortment of stove and greenhouse plants'. There were 31 stands of show leeks, 17 of pot leeks and 16 of celery. Mr R. Moore of Leamside was the judge and, for pot leeks, T. Rumford and E. Haswell took first and second place respectively. Readers will note the classification here of leeks into 'show' and 'pot'; unlike previous reports which mentioned only 'leeks'.

In 1905 Brandon Village held its fourth leek show. A room was made available at the Bay Horse Inn and this was decorated with streamers, Japanese lanterns and bunting. At the Red Lion Inn at nearby Brandon Colliery the decoration seems to have been quite a spectacle. The leeks were displayed on a large table in the centre of the room. Over this table, three arches of evergreens were formed, from which hung bunches of mountain ash berries. The walls themselves were adorned with sprays of evergreens, and flags were strung across the room. It was this particular show which inspired me to revive the tradition of decorating the room for the 1980 National Pot Leek Show. The Alexandra at Grangetown was the venue, and yew branches and rowan berries graced the pillared walls; the plant material was by courtesy of the Lambton estate. A five-foot-tall table centre-piece was created by Mrs A. Longfellow, flower arranger of Cleadon Village, and this included yew, laurel, chrysanthemums and apples. Flags and bunting were loaned by Vaux Breweries and (in place of Japanese lanterns) balloons were used, for safety (*Figure 1*). The centre table was 100 feet long and 8 feet wide and there were two side tables, each 50 feet long and 4 feet wide. Three hundred and ninety-two leeks were staged from 196 stands. This was the biggest leek show ever! That same year, for comparison, the other top shows had the following stands:

Bass Show, Seaburn	31 stands (62 leeks)
Sanderson, Morpeth	30 stands (60 leeks)
Newcastle Brown, Ashington	19 stands (57 leeks) ⎫ three in a stand
Evening Chronicle, Newcastle	16 stands (48 leeks) ⎭

Leek shows have always been highly competitive and attempts are sometimes made to ensure that certain individuals do not enter the show. At its worst, this includes vandalizing the leeks while they are still growing, but more often exclusion is to be found in the show schedule, with the words 'members only'.

As long ago as 1895, at Langley Moor, 30 members of the newly formed leek club held their first show at the Railway Inn. Even then, regulations were enforced to prevent leeks from a distance being shown in the members' class. Nevertheless, it was wisely determined to have a class open to all comers; here, leeks of enormous proportions were on view. Some, measuring 8 inches in circumference and proportionate in length, resembled pit props (as an enthusiastic pitman remarked). By comparison, the leeks in the members' class were about the thickness of a clothes peg and blanched to about the length of that article! The reporter was forced to make some comment and I think he showed great diplomacy by stating that the leeks in the all-comers class showed the members of the Society, and amateurs in the art of gardening, that 'the art of leek growing can be developed by assiduous attention and the proper cultivation of the soil'. Incidentally, the three prizewinners (and I presume these are for the members' class) were J. Bell, who received a china tea set; W. Willis, who had trousers made to measure, and J. Milner, who received a steel fender.

3

Pot Leeks in the North East — The Formative Years

The distinction between other leeks and a pot leek is not clearly defined. For guidance, the exhibitor must look at the show schedule, which will clearly state the length of the blanch area. Today there are more 'six-inch shows' than any other, and this length has largely been the tradition of County Durham. However, in Northumberland, '5½-inch shows' still exist, although there is a movement away from this to enable the exhibitor to compete on equal terms at the 'open shows' which predominantly require 6 inches. One show, the ill-fated 'Sanderson' at Morpeth (see pages 90–91), did attempt a brave compromise at 5¾ inches!

Completely out of step (and for reasons only known to themselves), the National Vegetable Society show schedule for open classes at the Harrogate Great Autumn Show of 1982 stipulated a 7 inch length of blanch! There is a tendency now for the pot leek to be upwards of 6 inches, for intermediate to be from this to 14 inches, and for the long leek to be in excess of this.

It is hard to believe that such confusion has existed for decades, with little effort being made to sort it out until recently. The main reason for a determined effort now is to prevent the demise of the long leek; in the north, even these are measured by cubic capacity as a major part of the judging. Some long leek classes were being won with very fat 'pot' leeks that had become too long for their entry into a pot leek class. Leeks of 8, 9 and 10 inches with a huge circumference had a much greater volume than well-grown truly 'long' leeks of much smaller circumference. The solution was to have three classes; pot, intermediate and long.

The confusion that must have existed at the turn of the century and beyond can only be guessed at. In the last century leeks seemed to have been judged by a measure of their length and girth — there are many examples where the sizes are recorded and the pattern appears to be to denote the length first. In 1895 at 'The Cousins', Gilesgate, the leeks shown were 12 × 6 inches and in 1896 they were 8½ × 6¼ inches. In 1899 at the 'Angel Inn', Crossgate, H. MacKnight won with a trio which looked the most level; their measurements were 9½ × 5½, 9½ × 5½ and 9 × 5 inches. In 1903 the 'Star' leek club had the best leek measuring 11 × 6 inches while at the 'Stag's Head', Esh Winning, 12 × 5½ inches was measured.

At Silksworth in 1900 the annual leek and vegetable show was opened in the Drill Hall and Mr R. Moore of Leamside was the judge. Twenty-eight prizes were awarded for spring leeks, six for pot leeks, three for celery, cauliflowers and beet and two for carrots, parsnips and red cabbage. The prize winners for pot leeks were W. Elliott, H. Humm, L. Turnbull, W. Munday, J. Pattison and M. Elliott. No pot leeks were recorded as being exhibited in 1898 or 1899.

In 1901 members of the Silksworth Colliery leek club held their show at the Volunteer Drill Hall. Mr R. Moore of Leamside was the judge once more and there were 27 stands of leeks, 14 of pot leeks and 11 of celery. The prizewinners for pot leeks were, in order of merit: J. Pattison, jr; J. Pattison, sr; W. Elliott; L. Ridley; W. Simpson; M. Elliot and J. Robson.

In 1902 there was a pot leek show at Low Spennymoor and another at Leamside where there were 30 entries. Money prizes were offered and also a silver medal for first place, that was won by T. Patterson of Silksworth; second was W. Hodgson of Plawsworth and third, Mr Walt of Leamside. A large number of people attended this show and the general opinion expressed was that it was 'one of the best held that season'. Incidentally, at the National show in 1980 I, too, provided a silver medal for the prizewinner and in addition a bronze medal for every stand over 110 cubic inches, anticipating but a few. The show broke almost every record: 13 stands over 120 cubic inches, 22 over 110 cubic inches and 27 over 100 cubic inches; a stand was for two leeks).

Fifty competitors entered the club show held in 1902 at Mr A. Hope's hostelry, the 'Puddlers' Arms', Low Spennymoor. Mr M. Yare of Wolsingham was the judge and £3 was offered in prizes. The record states that the first three were as follows: J. Mounsey, 15s (75p); J. Nelson, 10s (50p); T. Jefferson, 7s 6d (37½p).

In 1903 pot leeks appeared at the Langley Park annual show, which was held on a field near the church. It was the seventh year of this exhibition and, with 2025 entries, it was considered the largest and most important in the county. The prizes for the best pot leeks went to J. Turnbull, W. Burr, J. Harris and J. Stobbs.

Also in 1903, an open leek and vegetable show was held at Mr Ben Wright's 'Commercial Inn', Hetton-le-Hole. Being an 'open' show it attracted the attention of leek growers all over the county and as a result a splendid entry was secured. J. Wilson of Moorsley won first prize, followed by T. Thompson of Hetton-le-Hole and M. Oliver of Houghton-le-Spring. Other exhibits were cauliflowers, parsnips, red cabbage, celery, beet and show leeks.

To make a distinction between pot leeks and other leeks, alternative names had to be found: 'show leeks' as described at the Commercial Inn seems inappropriate; 'spring leeks' was an alternative more frequently used. Today some exhibitors talk of long leeks, blanch leeks and trench leeks, meaning leeks other than 'pot'. I believe the distinction will eventually be fixed at pot, intermediate and long.

In 1906 at the 'Bush Inn', Washington Village, an open show was held where the blanch area was limited to 6 inches in length. There were 47 stands and the leeks in first place measured 76 cubic inches, those in second place, 71 cubic inches, and those in third measured 68 cubic inches. There is no record of the number that comprised a stand in this show.

Sacriston regarded themselves as pioneers of leek clubs and they held their ninth annual show at the 'Robin Hood Inn' in 1906. No mention is made of the type of leek exhibited. In the same year the seventh 'Murton Colliery' leek show was held at the Miners' Hall which was 'tastefully decorated' for the occasion. The judge, Mr T. Richardson, was superintendent of Ryhope Cemetery. Pot leeks were not to exceed 5½ inches in length, and three comprised a stand. C. Wills, T. Metcalfe, R. Norman and J. Short were the winners for this class.

In 1907 the Victoria Leek and Celery show of Murton Colliery was held in the concert hall of the Workmen's Club and Institute; the judge was Mr T. Marsden of Fatfield. Prizes were supplied by Murton Colliery Co-operative Society and pot leeks were not to exceed 5 inches in length. M. White, J. Laidler and B. Elliott were the prizewinners in the open class. A specific pot leek show was held at Thinford, near Spennymoor and was promoted by Mr G. Atkinson. Twenty-seven competitors sought prize money totalling over £3 and the prizewinners were J. Evans, J. Joyce and W. Joyce. Also in 1907, members of the Silksworth Workmen's Club held their annual pot leek show. Mr R. Willis of Millfield judged and awards, in order of merit, went to W. Latham, G. Horsley, S. Johnson and W. Carter.

In 1909 the Dalton-le-Dale Leek and Celery Society held their third annual show at the 'Times Inn' by courtesy of the host, Mr J.R. Watson. The judge Mr C. Brown officiated and a stand comprised two pot leeks not to exceed 5 inches in length. W. Marley, J. Shipley and T. Waddell were the prizewinners. In the same year, members of the Page Bank pot leek club held their annual show at the house of Mrs M.E. Simpson, Shafto Arms, Page Bank. There was a large entry and exhibits 'were remarkable for their excellent quality' making the task of judging by Mr J.T. Lawson of Page Bank a difficult one. The winners were C. Usher, junior, J. Stanworth and T. Marley, junior. At Shotley Bridge in 1909 the best leek in the show (held in the Co-operative Hall) was 40 cubic inches and second 34 cubic inches. The winners were J. Forster and J. Moore respectively. A late show was held at the hostelry of Mr J. Spears of the 'Smith's Arms', Gilesgate in 1909. The room was, once again, 'tastefully decorated' by members of the committee! Thirty-three entries were received from the members of the 'Cousins' Leek and Celery Club'. A silver challenge cup and a gold medal were awarded to T. Norwood for leeks of 104 cubic inches. J. Brown and G. Perry were placed second and third respectively by the judge, Mr T. Stewart of Crossgate (pot leeks were not specified nor the number comprising a stand). Again in 1909, 84.12 cubic inches won the 'Oswald Hedley' cup at Southmoor — there were 69 stands and J. Armstrong was the prizewinner. This was possibly for a pair of pot leeks, but the report did not make this clear. While cubic inches are frequently being mentioned, a leek and celery show held at 'The Angel', Crossgate, was won by an entry of 13 × 6 inches, as was the pattern a decade previous.

In 1910, at Mrs Rutherford's 'Beehive Hotel', Willington, there was a good show of pot leeks, beet, celery and red cabbage. Mr T. Foster was judge and R. Proud won with 63 cubic inches, J.W. Scratcher second with 57¼ and J. Wilkinson third with 54 cubic inches; the size of stand is not recorded. The cubic capacity of the second-prize winning stand draws attention to the fact that measuring tables and equipment in eighths of an inch were used until 1979 — the year in which the 'Calderbank Standards' of accuracy were introduced. These included an accurate tool to measure the length of blanch, computer-accurate tables (see pages 103–110) and a fibreglass tape (that could not be stretched!) for measuring the circumference of the leeks. All these were in tenths of an inch and, within months, judges were using this new equipment for greater accuracy. Judges should remember to include the veil of the leek when measuring the length of blanch (*Figure 2*).

In 1911 the first pot leek show in connection with the New Brancepeth Club and Institute Ltd took place. Mr G. Swan was the judge and the show was open to all members and affiliated associations. Eighteen stands of leeks were evident and the prizewinners were: J. Bell, 15s (75p); R. Charlton, 10s (50p); W. Finlay, 5s (25p).

Another first show at Springwell in connection with the Workmen's Club and Institute was held in 1912 where there were 62 exhibits, first places going to T. Humphrey of Washington Village, J. Mitchinson, Usworth and A. Smith, also of Usworth. In the same year, Meadowfield and District Workmen's Club held their first pot leek show of 41 stands: prizewinners were R. McKnight (gold medal and table cover), H. Martin (silver medal and eiderdown quilt) and J. Mullinger (pair of pictures and pair of trousers). Also in 1912, Mr J. Abbott carried off premier honours at the Washington Village Workmen's Club annual pot leek show. The successful leeks were sent to Durham City where they were exhibited in the Town Hall at the Durham County Clubs' Union Show; here they secured seventh prize. The tradition of sending the prizewinning leeks on to the Durham County Clubs' Union Show continues and because the latter is a show of 'champions' it is often well worthy of a visit. The leeks are marginally past their best, having been on two show benches, but they are all equal in that respect. At the 'County Show', as it is known, the exhibits are entered under the name of the club and not that of the individual exhibitor.

Pot leeks were a 'special feature' of the 1914 show held at the 'Blue Bell Hotel', Willington. Mr T. Foster, junior, was judge and the prizewinners were A. Alder with 99 cubic inches, Mrs Plumpton, also with 99 cubic inches, and W. Daley, with 96 cubic inches; whether the stand was for two or for three leeks was not recorded. Also in 1914, the second pot leek show was held at South Hetton Workmen's Club; Mr D. Headen of Hetton Downs was the judge and two ladies featured in the top three! Mrs R. Smithson won with a stand of 54 cubic inches, Mr J. Hall was second, with 52 cubic inches and Mrs J. Hall was third with 52½ cubic inches; £100 was given in prizes. It is noteworthy that the largest leeks do not always win because the size forms only a part of the judging. Although Mrs Hall's leeks were larger, they must have been marginally of poorer quality than those of her husband. The extent to which size is important is discussed in the chapter on judging (pages 81–83).

In 1916 pot leeks became a feature of the Sherburn Jubilee Leck Club which had its first leek show in 1910. The show was held at the house of Mr E. Davis, 'Grey Horse Inn', Sherburn; the prizewinners were G. West, senior, S. West, and T. Bewick.

Researching through old newspapers with their large format, small print and lack of photographs, although intriguing, can also be monotonous and boring. It can also be frustrating, when one sentence appears to be full of promise, yet leads nowhere. For example, in 1902, a report mentioned that there was a 'new scheme' for running a leek show on lines different from those in a public house. Just what this was is not known to me: could it have been the use of cubic inches, or perhaps restriction of length of blanch to 5, 5½ or 6 inches?

4

Pot Leeks — Nation-Wide

The first pair of leeks that I exhibited reached 124 cubic inches and this was my first season in the mid 1970s. I came second at the show, which required three leeks; my third leek was so unlike the other two that I lost valuable points. In retrospect I was fortunate to have done so well, having grown a total of only seven leeks. The following year I took the red ticket, but I knew by then that exhibiting was not going to be a personal interest of mine.

I was more motivated to making the pot leek a national vegetable in the sense that it would be more widely grown and exhibited. In addition, I was appalled that so many shows were being won by the same exhibitors. These were winning shows, not so much because of their greater knowledge, but because they had a better leek — one they would not share. I decided that I would always distribute my knowledge and my plants to make exhibiting more equal and the pot leek more widely grown.

The disease, rust (*Puccinia porri*) (see pages 70–71) was prevalent in the North East and exhibitors had little idea about what it was and how to prevent it; those who did know were not telling! I decided to put the record straight by holding a meeting in the hope that those in attendance would return to their clubs and inform others.

In order to attract leek growers I held the first 'Pot Leek Symposium' at Monkwearmouth College of Further Education in Sunderland. It was to be held on the morning of Saturday 28 January 1978 and tickets were 40 p each. Maureen Doherty of Leeds University had made a special study of leek rust and I invited her to speak at the symposium. Dr J.T. Fletcher of the Ministry of Agriculture also agreed to attend and answer questions on other leek diseases. I spoke in the main about growing mediums and fertilizers and George Stonehouse, a well-known exhibitor and judge, gave a talk on how he raised leeks.

The occasion was a huge success and it was our good fortune that the firemen were on strike, otherwise the hall would not have been allowed to accommodate so many! There were no aisles, as nearly 400 squeezed together in a room suitable for only half that number. The event was well publicized, both locally and nationally, and people arrived on the day from all over the North East, Cumbria and Border regions.

The symposium was used to introduce the formation of a Pot Leek Society, and a leaflet giving details of this was distributed. This Society was the first attempt to draw together all the individual club members, to share knowledge and leek plants, but in particular to broaden the area in which pot leeks were being grown. For £2.00 each member would receive a journal published four times each year, a plastic membership card and a reduced-price soil-analysis service, and could also take advantage of other special offers on fertilizers, growing mediums, etc. Plants would be made available and there would be an annual show which was free to enter. A badge at 80p including postage was soon made available. The first 200 members would be known as founder members and their membership card stated this. It took four months to recruit the founder members and I learned that unless something is free then it was going to take a lot of selling!

It was fortunate that I was writing at the time for *Amateur Gardening* and, through articles on pot leeks here, and later in *Garden News* and *Gardening World*, I soon created an interest in other parts of the country. I was giving talks and slide shows at various leek clubs and held the second pot leek symposium in the Berryhill and District British Legion Club, West Midlands, on the morning of Saturday 29 April 1978.

The first show of the Pot Leek Society was held on 30 September in Sunderland at the same college. It was a disappointment to me, with so few stands and even fewer spectators. First prize was £25.00 and the 'Echo' trophy; second £15.00 and third £10.00. The sponsor for the show was the *Echo*, Sunderland and the judge G. Stonehouse.

The first ten places were as follows:

A. Murray	Quebec	111.9 cubic inches/pair
T. Little	Houghton-le-Spring	104.5
A. Dodd	Ovingham	89.8
G. Murray	Consett	105.2
J. Kelly	Durham	83.4
J. Fell	Carlisle	94.8
J. Duxfield	Consett	88.6
R. Wylie	Sunderland	101.8
J. Soulsby	Birtley	77.7
J. Robson	Blyth	90.7

T. Little in second place, and hopeful of a win, had joined the Society three days earlier. The ruling today is that membership must be made on or before 1 June prior to the show. I, myself, fail to see the relevance of this and would personally welcome anyone up to the evening prior to the show.

Following these events I made a few appearances on television and radio in connection with pot leeks: a Tyne Tees presenter gave me the title of 'Professor of Pot Leeks' which has been quoted ever since!

Dr J. Fletcher was interested in the incidence of virus in leeks and I was able to obtain some plants for him to study. Leek virus, although unrecorded up to that time in Britain, is in fact endemic and present in all leeks (see pages 72–73). However, local newspapers and television gave the usual alarmist reports and in return the Society gained more publicity.

It was a hard, uphill task recruiting members. I found that running the Society single-handed demanded all my spare time: my own leek growing and other interests declined dramatically. An article I wrote for the first journal included the use of 'Perlite' in the growing medium and this article was reproduced and distributed by the suppliers, Silvaperl Products Ltd. This not only helped to increase their sales but was mutually beneficial in that the leaflet advertised the existence of the Society to all parts of Britain.

Members increasingly asked whether leek plants could be supplied through the Society. I was introduced by J.R. Duxfield, a founder member, to G.M. Murray of Derwent Nurseries. Mr Murray had won the Bass show (see pages 88–89) in 1976 with 149.12 cubic inches. The leeks offered to the Society were known as the 'MM' and had been developed from the more well known 'TL' leek. A total of 1704 leeks raised in pots and 384 raised in boxes were ordered. A dozen in 5 inch pots cost members £9.50 and in boxes £5.50 — the 50p in each case went to Society funds. Unfortunately, for various reasons this project was not a success.

In 1979 I raised my biggest single leek, which measured 75 cubic inches; it was short and a little corrugated, but had I had two in the trench I would have stood a better chance in the Society show. This was held at the Grindon Mill, Sunderland, by courtesy of Vaux breweries who became joint sponsors with the *Echo*, Sunderland. I was hopeful of a good show, for 1979 had gone quite well (apart from the 'MM' leeks) and I knew that if a show of some calibre could materialize, the Society was on an upward trend. Mr G. Stonehouse was judge once again and soon after midnight on the Friday evening the results were known. Eighty-six stands of two leeks made an impressive start; in addition there was quality to be found, as well as quantity.

In 1978 the first 20 stands had totalled 1658.8 cubic inches; in 1979 the figure for the same number of leeks was 2255.2 cubic inches — a 36% increase. Prize money in 1979 was £130.00, £25.00 and £15.00, with trade prizes being offered down to 26th place (in 1978 the first 13 received a prize). I named the show the 'National' and the Society became the 'National Pot Leek Society' (*Figure 3*).

The first ten places were as follows:

W. Mould	Darlington	146.7 cubic inches/pair
W. Maires	Bishop Auckland	139.3
J. Greasley	Bishop Auckland	138.0
A. Murray	Quebec	121.0
J. Wright	Bellingham	118.1
J. Thompson	Spennymoor	108.4
J. French	Sacriston	115.1
J. Wanless	Wark	104.8
T. Little	Fencehouses	107.0
D.A. Calderbank	Bournmoor	104.6

I was delighted to creep into the top ten, particularly so that I could prove the point that quality does count: the leeks entered by J.R. Duxfield, who came eleventh, measured 116.2 cubic inches and were bigger than mine. However, my own stand had no point deductions: they were perfect, and as a result gained a higher position than the larger leeks of four other exhibitors. Size is not everything.

The 1979 show attracted many top names in the exhibitors' world including Walter Wilson, famous for the 'Nine Pin' leeks. Unfortunately, he was disqualified because his leeks were slightly too long, which was an unusual slip for a leek grower and judge of his calibre.

During October I published the first booklet on pot leeks; it was inexpensive and, although small, had a national circulation, helping to promote pot leeks. The publication also included computer-accurate measuring tables in the new tenths of an inch for greater accuracy (see pages 103–110). An unstretchable tape measure and measuring tool completed the equipment needed by a judge and they were known as the 'Calderbank Standards'. Local newspapers referred to the book as the leek growers' 'Bible'!

The week after the National show I heard of a pair of record-size pot leeks being shown at Ouston Social Club, Perkinsville, Co. Durham. The judge had measured one at 100 cubic inches and the second at 94.3 cubic inches; the previous record for a pair had been held by N. Hughes of Blackhall in 1975 with a stand of 180.15 cubic inches. This new record provided the publicity that I needed to secure more members and to encourage present members to renew their subscriptions — particularly as the cost of membership was rising to £3.00 per annum! The problem was that although the current record holder, A. Herbert, was a member of the Society, his winning leeks were going unnoticed by the Press. I contacted the local press and sent one of their photographs to *Garden News*: this publication gave the story good coverage and in turn I got an exclusive story for the yearbook — which was available to new members and to those renewing their subscriptions!

By the end of 1979 the National Pot Leek Society had an 'information bureau' and such distinguishing features as its own tie, letter-headed notepaper, etc. Bob Woolley, the gardening correspondent well known in the rose world, joined the Society and commented that I was 'the first person who has managed to bring pot leek enthusiasts together in unanimity'! The hard work was beginning to pay off; advertisers for the Society publications were no longer difficult to find and W. Richardson of Chempak fertilizers became another major cash sponsor for the 1980 show.

Early in 1980 a leaflet was printed by Phostrogen, as one of a series on raising plants using their fertilizer. This was entitled 'Pot and Blanch Leeks by D.A. Calderbank with a guide to feeding by J.R. Duxfield'. Although I could not claim that I had used this fertilizer alone, my co-author had used it and was happy to be included. This leaflet enhanced my desire to make pot leeks nationally grown, by making them available free of charge and by advertising their existence in gardening publications.

Walter Maires of Evenwood provided plants for 1980 and, remembering the disappointments of the previous season, I asked members to contact him directly should they be dissatisfied in any way; Walter Wilson also provided plants. Clubs were being affiliated to the National Society and bronze and silver medals were struck to award at shows. The silver was to be awarded by a registered judge only, although as there was no test this did not effectively become a measure of excellence as had been hoped.

During 1980, membership began to climb rapidly and it was becoming difficult to answer letters by return of post which I had always aimed to do. I decided to withdraw from the active running of the Society and the 1980 show was to be my 'swan song'. The show was free to enter; first prize was £500.00, a silver medal and the *Echo* trophy; second £150.00 and a bronze medal and third £75.00 and a bronze medal. Every stand over 110 cubic inches would also get a bronze medal and there were many trade prizes for lower places. The 'Alexandra', Grangetown, Sunderland was to be the venue and the judge Mr F.C. Palmer of Stamfordham. The room was decorated in the traditional way (see *Figure 1*) and 'Marshalls Seeds' promised a packet of exhibition sweet pea seed to every entrant.

On the evening of Friday 19 September the members started to arrive with their leeks, in such numbers that a queue developed as exhibitors arrived faster than stewards could take their leeks and place them on the tables. By

8 p.m. 392 leeks occupied the centre table measuring 100 × 8 ft plus two side tables of 50 × 4 ft. The room was rather dimly lit and the observer standing at one end of the room gained the impression that the leeks were stretching away into infinity; a truly impressive sight!

Faced with this abundance, the judge had an impossible task: I therefore recruited some members of the Society who were recognized judges. We all measured the leeks and arranged them in order of size. This took something like four hours to complete; everyone then left except for the judge and myself! By the early hours of the morning all the leeks had been placed except for those in the first and second positions.

The biggest leeks were those of D. Smiles at 155.51 cubic inches (*Figure 4*): the next in size were those of A. Waite, at 146.57 cubic inches (*Figure 5*). The bigger leeks did not have that pristine appearance of the slightly smaller ones; they, perhaps, had been lifted on Thursday evening, thus losing a little lustre. I believe that a small amount of soil was also evident deep inside the roots. The judge deducted a total of 10 points, placing the biggest leeks in second place, but the prizewinner was not to know by what a narrow margin he won!

The 1980 show had quality as well as size: this was shown by the fact that Tom Fenton, a respected vegetable exhibitor and winner at Southport Flower Show, did not even appear in the top fifty! The first twenty stands totalled 2549.14 cubic inches — an increase of 13% on the 1979 show and 54% on the 1978 show. Mr E. Raydon, three times winner of the *News of the World* show, and highly respected judge, came out of retirement to enter this show and gained thirteenth position. D. Cooper, who came second in the Bass show in 1979, reached eleventh place, while W. Mould, National winner in 1979, came twenty-third and A. Murray, winner in 1978, was thirtieth!

The first ten winners were as follows:

A. Waite	Cramlington	146.57 cubic inches/pair
D. Smiles	Eighton Banks	155.51
T. Elgie	Wolsingham	137.35
D. Alderson	Blyth	133.18
T. Little	Fencehouses	132.04
J. Soulsby	Birtley	135.89
J.T. Harrison	Newbottle	124.99
F. Bennett	Durham	123.65
J. Jones	Stanhope	121.26

I always insisted that the prizewinner should receive his cheque in person from the sponsor at the presentation itself. Too many exhibitors are entering shows while they are acting as judges elsewhere, so that they are absent from the prizegiving ceremony. I feel that this is ill-mannered: it was not allowed to happen at any show that I organized, or it was stipulated that the prizemoney would be withheld. However, the ceremony went well in 1980 and gained coverage on local television. The show ended with lectures given by Dr J.T. Fletcher and myself. At this point J. Soulsby was introduced as the Chairman of the Society, and I 'bowed out'. At the time of my 'retirement' there were exactly 700 members: a year later there were 595 members.

There had been criticisms of how the Society had been run and I must admit that to run a national society single-handed is unusual. However, decisions can be made quickly when there is no committee and, in the initial years, this was essential otherwise there would have been no Society! One criticism was that the top growers were not attracted to the Society: however, this was nonsense, and I was able to refute the allegation by reference to some of the members, for example:

A. Herbert	'World' record holder (2) leeks
T. Little	County champion
A. Atkinson	County champion
R. Bell	'World' record holder (1) leek (*Guinness Book of Records*)
J. Davidson	'Kestrel Lager' and 'Bass' champion
E. Raydon	*News of the World* champion
D. Smiles	Biggest leeks exhibited in 1980

Other illustrious members included W. Maires, D. Cooper, J.R. Greasley, T.R. Elgie, W. Bird, R. Brown, T. Fenton, A. Murray, W. Mould and A. Waite.

I had also been criticized for my strong views on judging and judges: *Garden News* subsequently published a major article on this topic. It is my opinion that most shows are judged inadequately and I feel that even the 'Open' shows have been 'open' to question!

Having relinquished the organization and running of the Society, I had much more time to devote to my own pursuits. In mid-1981 I produced my latest aid to growing pot leeks, a cassette tape, which explained the cultivation and exhibiting of these vegetables. Although it achieved only a moderate success it was another 'first' for me, preceding the tape produced by Robinsons of Forton which included pot leeks and which appeared in 1982.

Later in 1981 I was judge at the Stourbridge Pot Leek Society show and became their President from 1981 to 1982; this was the largest show in the

Midlands. A few weeks later the 1982 edition of Marshalls' seed catalogue appeared and it included a leek supplied by myself and named after my son, Elliot. This leek was known as 'Elliot's Original' and sold so well that, although this was the 1982 catalogue, Marshalls had sold out of leek plants by the end of November 1981. This was the first time that leek plants had been offered by a national seed company. Although I had supplied stock plants in late 1979 to Ward and Newton of Richmond, I understand that these were for experimental use at a laboratory in an attempt to find a way of eradicating the endemic virus disease, before plants were sold to the public.

In 1980 I had begun to distribute seed and information on the cultivation of pot leeks; over 500 packets were distributed in three seasons. The destinations and number of packets gives an indication of the growth of interest in pot leeks:

Tyne & Wear	147	Somerset	2
Co. Durham	108	Berkshire	2
Cumbria	42	Suffolk	2
West Midlands	37	Powys	2
Cleveland	33	Essex	2
Northumberland	28	Cheshire	1
N. Yorkshire	21	Gwent	1
Borders	19	Dorset	1
Lancashire	18	Wiltshire	1
Staffordshire	18	S. Glamorgan	1
Warwickshire	17	Dumfries & Galloway	1
Nottinghamshire	11	Cornwall	1
Strathclyde	9	Avon	1
W. Yorkshire	8	Middlesex	1
S. Yorkshire	8	Lothian	1
Hampshire	7	Surrey	1
Kent	7	Guernsey	1
Shropshire	5	Fife	1
Mid Glamorgan	4	W. Glamorgan	1
Hertfordshire	4	Devon	1
Humberside	3	Shetland	1
Tayside	3	Lincolnshire	1
Isle of Man	2	Clwyd	1
Derbyshire	2	Highlands	1
Dyfed	2		

This list represents only those who have received seed from me; I am confident that where the seed has been grown successfully there will be an upsurge of interest in that area. As the list indicates, leek growing is by no means restricted to the North East: a pot leek club exists at Chard in Somerset and others are becoming established elsewhere, including the South. E.F. Newman of Portsmouth, using my seed, developed a lot of local interest by being so successful at his show. In 1982 he gained a Royal Horticultural Society bronze model and diploma in excellence for horticulture, his leeks being the best single vegetable exhibit in the whole show. Pot leeks soon pass from being a novelty on the showbench to a challenge that few growers can resist.

A letter I received from S.C. Love of Bristol in 1982 requesting seed said 'I intend to create an interest at our "Bristol Corporation Show" to encourage other exhibitors to show them'. This is now the way that pot leeks will become more popular, both for raising and for exhibition.

As well as seed, I have also distributed plants. I have been delighted that these have won many shows for exhibitors. The following are a few examples:

D. Smiles at the Stormont Main Club, Wrekenton, had wins in 1980, 1981 and 1982 with 169.90, 139.5 and 160 cubic inches per pair. The only person to have won this show for three years in succession was R. Willey in 1977, 1978 and 1979 with his own leeks measuring 108, 91 and 116 cubic inches. D. Smiles also came second in the National in 1980 with 155.51 cubic inches/pair and first in 1981 with 112.8 at the Half Moon Hotel, Wrekenton.

R. Matthison won at the Springwell Club Show in 1980 with leeks measuring 148.00 cubic inches/pair and in 1981 with 118 cubic inches/pair; he also won at the Rickleton Club with 100 cubic inches/pair.

J. Soulsby won the Cramlington Open in 1980 with leeks measuring 136.52 cubic inches/pair, and was awarded a Royal Horticultural Society bronze medal for quality.

J. Carr, in 1980, with leeks measuring 142.89 cubic inches/pair, won the Half Moon Hotel show: in that same year W.J. Douglas won at Thorney Close Workmen's Club with 135.64 cubic inches/pair; J. Reid won at East Herrington with 127.00 cubic inches/pair, and the latter also won at the Seaham Show with 123.7 cubic inches/pair.

In 1981 T. Edgar won the Longtown Social Club show in Carlisle with 105 cubic inches/pair. In 1982 H. Tate won the Glendale with 124 cubic inches/pair and D. Johnson won at Grangetown with leeks of 141 cubic inches/pair.

Other wins with my leeks have included one for a seedling of 63 cubic inches for one, exhibited by E. Walker of Gateshead, and many wins in the Midlands by W. Holmes and others.

Pot leeks are now a nationally recognized, nationally grown and nationally exhibited vegetable. The 'migration' of some north-eastern miners to other mining areas, notably the Midlands, has had some influence in this respect. However, it is the events from 1978 onwards, which have been described in this chapter and which are summarized in chronological order below, that have been largely responsible for the increased nation-wide interest in pot leeks:

January 1978	Pot leek symposium held at Sunderland; formation of the Pot Leek Society.
April 1978	Pot leek symposium held in the Midlands.
September 1978	Pot Leek Society show held at Monkwearmouth College, Sunderland.
1979	Leaflet on pot leeks distributed by Silvaperl Products.
May 1979	Distribution of pot leek plants to Society members.
September 1979	National Pot Leek Society show held at the Grindon Mill, Sunderland.
September 1979	'World' record leeks grown by a Society member.
September 1979	First show with a £1000 prize — the Sanderson show.
October 1979	First pot leek book published, written by D.A. Calderbank.
February 1980	Leaflet on pot leeks distributed by Phostrogen Ltd and written by D.A. Calderbank and J.R. Duxfield.
February 1980	Distribution of pot leek plants to Society members.
September 1980	National show held at the Alexandra, Sunderland — biggest and best pot leek show ever staged!
November 1980	Started the distribution of seed to all parts of Britain.
June 1981	First cassette tape published on raising and showing pot leeks.
1982	Marshalls' Seeds introduced the pot leek 'Elliot's Original', supplied by D.A. Calderbank.

I have been delighted by the upsurge of interest in the growing and exhibiting of pot leeks and, in order to maintain and encourage this trend I have written more articles on the subject of pot leeks, in gardening periodicals from 1978 onwards, than probably any other author! That I have subsequently appeared on television and in local and national radio programmes, and also have had the honour to be invited to give illustrated lectures to numerous clubs and societies, may perhaps be taken as a measure of the interest generated.

SECTION TWO

This looks in detail at the methods of raising all types of leek. Beginning with the choice of greenhouse, it then examines every aspect of leek cultivation and propagation, ending with a comprehensive account of the pests, problems and diseases that may be encountered and how to overcome them.

5

The Greenhouse

A greenhouse is essential for raising exhibition leeks; electric propagators and window ledges are of very limited value. If you are unable to use a greenhouse then I would recommend that you purchase the leek plants in May from a recognized grower.

Any greenhouse, whatever the design or structural material, will be suitable for growing leeks. As it is unlikely that you will be growing leeks only, you should take all factors into consideration before selecting your greenhouse. Nevertheless, whatever your choice, any greenhouse that is to be used for raising leeks must incorporate certain essential features, and these are discussed in the next few pages.

LIGHT

The greenhouse must allow light to enter and reach the plants; although this sounds fundamental to all greenhouses, in practice it is often far from being the case.

To maximize on available light, a greenhouse should be positioned with the main spar in a west-to-east direction. The sun will then shine on the long side and not just on a gable end. This is especially important in the early months of the year when the winter sun is weak, low in the sky, and not always visible!

Older wooden greenhouses with their smaller glass panes do not allow as much light to enter as the more modern aluminium greenhouses with their narrow support structures and larger panes of glass. Both types will help you to produce good leeks but it is important to keep the glass clean, particularly that of the older models. An annual cleaning of glass may be enough in the most rural areas but more frequent cleaning will be needed elsewhere.

Industrial pollution is a potential hazard to all greenhouses to some degree as the film of grime that settles on the glass inhibits light. A fortnightly wash is essential from January to the end of May in these industrial areas.

Heavy rainfall does not clean glass sufficiently well but a hosepipe and brush attachment will make short work of an otherwise demanding task. A few minutes is all that is required; there is no need to dry the glass, and, if time is at a premium, wash only the south-facing side.

DRAUGHT-PROOFING

There should be no serious draughts in the greenhouse. Loose-seated glass should be corrected and any cracked or missing panes replaced. A draught around the door can be minimized by placing a piece of heavy-duty polythene sheeting behind the door.

To check the efficiency of your greenhouse draught-proofing, choose a windy day and take a candle and a box of matches into the greenhouse. Secure the door and polythene sheeting and move the lighted candle around the interior, holding it close to the glass. Obviously, if the flame goes out this indicates that there is a draught which will cause heat loss; in the ideal greenhouse the flame should hardly flicker, even when the strongest of winds is blowing outside.

When using the 'candle test' it is important to turn the greenhouse heating off first, for otherwise this will create convection currents that would cause the flame to move. It is also useful to perform the test during the evening as the flame will be more evident in the dark than in daylight.

STRUCTURE

The ideal greenhouse for raising leeks specifically would have a solid base up to the height of the interior staging. The base may be of brick, wood, concrete, or any other solid structure. Home-made greenhouses may make use of breeze blocks to form a solid wall quickly.

Solid-based greenhouses conserve heat and, as leeks are raised on the staging, there is no advantage in having glass beneath that height. In addition, greenhouses constructed with glass right down to the ground require more heat to maintain a high temperature because of heat losses through the glass.

Polythene greenhouses are poor insulators, are expensive to heat and have a poor light transmission. Condensation is a problem not easily overcome and this further inhibits the light intake. However, polythene and glass-to-ground greenhouses may be used throughout the month of May when no artificial heat is required for raising the plants.

A greenhouse with a solid base wall will not require any additional insulation. Polythene sheeting can be used on glass-to-ground greenhouses but this should not rise above the height of the staging on which the leeks are placed. The polythene will reduce heating costs by providing better insulation but if it is used above staging height it can cause problems for plant growth: ventilation becomes less efficient; humidity levels rise, as does the condensation, and light transmission diminishes drastically.

I prefer aluminium for the greenhouse structure, with wooden staging that stands separately and that can be removed annually for treatment with a timber preservative that is not harmful to plants.

VENTILATION

Ventilation in the greenhouse is important: still damp air promotes fungal diseases and is not beneficial to plant growth. Ventilation also reduces condensation by providing a change of air within the greenhouse. Automatic ventilators are of great assistance: they open and close according to changes in temperature within the greenhouse and provide ventilation when it might otherwise be difficult to do so.

SPACE

The idea that you should buy a greenhouse larger than you think you might actually need is fostered by some greenhouse salesmen, and perpetuated by all untidy greenhouse owners. Buy a quality greenhouse; keep it clean and meticulously tidy, and you will be able to buy smaller than you originally thought — and also save on heating as a result.

It is possible to utilize the maximum amount of greenhouse space by placing staging down both sides and also across the rear wall of the greenhouse. In a small one it is possible to raise many leeks to planting-out size.

HEATING

Heating the greenhouse is often governed by personal choice and economy, rarely by the requirements of the plants. Although good leeks have been raised in all forms of heating, certain forms of heat give better results than others.

Heating that also produces humidity and carbon dioxide is best: such types include gas (both natural and bottled), and paraffin. Two cylinders are required for bottled gas, with an operational change-over valve allowing the automatic release of gas from the full cylinder as the first becomes empty. However, the propane gas used in these cylinders is expensive, making this form of heating unpopular.

Natural gas is much more economical to run but it is then necessary for the greenhouse to be near a mains gas supply. Paraffin is readily available and easy to instal but requires frequent adjustment and refilling. Fumes from the smouldering wick of an extinguished paraffin heater are toxic to leeks.

Electric fan heaters create a very dry atmosphere; however, a tray of water placed near the heater so that the warm air blows over it will help to increase humidity. Electrically operated tubular heaters can be made more economical to run by attaching aluminium foil sheeting behind the tubes; heat will then be directed away from the wall upon which the tubes are secured, and into the greenhouse.

Solid fuel boilers are expensive to buy, and need frequent refuelling; temperature control is also difficult, as is also the case with paraffin. However, for practicality, these two systems are commonly used by allotment holders.

A maximum-and-minimum thermometer is an essential piece of equipment in any heated greenhouse, as it records the highest and lowest temperatures reached in the greenhouse over a given period of time. Setting the indices one day and checking them the next will record the lowest overnight temperature accurately. The heater thermostat or height of wick, if paraffin is used, can then be adjusted accordingly.

For greater accuracy, the thermometer should be suspended so that it is slightly above the staging but not too close to the source of heat.

During the day the temperature is likely to rise higher than required because of the extra heat provided by the sun. This is of less importance than the overnight temperature, provided that automatic ventilators are fitted to allow cooling and that the plants have sufficient moisture in the potting compost.

6

Leek Cultivation — In the Greenhouse

GROWING MEDIUMS AND FERTILIZERS FOR USE IN POTS

Proprietary composts are available and it is advisable for a novice to use them initially. It is also possible to make one's own compost, using the methods recommended by commercial manufacturers of fertilizers. In addition, growers may experiment by mixing a growing medium to an individual formula. This may sound a very attractive idea and it has given rise to the so-called 'magic formulae' of some exhibitors. However, the basic requirements of all growing mediums are that they should be well drained, but not excessively so, and should provide nourishment to the developing plants until supplementary fertilizers are used.

I firmly believe that the greenhouse period of leek development is of vital importance. Huge leeks in September cannot be produced by careful treatment only from June onwards! Too many growers fail by thinking that if they lavish care on the plants while in the trench, this will be sufficient to raise prizewinning specimens. This is far from the truth and the correct care of the plants must cover the whole growing period, from January to the showbench in September or October.

Pot leeks remain in the greenhouse for approximately five months and it amazes me how some growers deny their plants any supplementary feeding during that time. Five months is longer than some vegetables require to complete their total life cycle! The fertilizers in the potting compost will sustain the plants for some weeks, but not indefinitely.

I use liquid and foliar feeds to supply the essential plant foods. There are many such feeds, and it is worth experimenting to find one that you prefer.

The fertilizers which will be readily known to all gardeners are nitrogen (N), phosphates (P) and potash (K), and these are available as combined fertilizers in different proportions. It is possible to have, for example, a high nitrogen feed, which may be indicated as 3:1:1. The figures refer to nitrogen, phosphate and potash respectively and are always shown in that order. Similarly a low nitrogen feed would be indicated as 1:2:2.

The decision the leek grower has to make is which fertilizer to choose — high nitrogen, high phosphates, low potash, or any other combination. This problem is one of the most difficult to overcome when raising any exhibition plant.

Guidance is given by many commercial producers of fertilizers, leeks being grouped together with onions and root crops. However, I have seen fertilizers recommended which are described as 1:2:2 and 1:1:3; although these are not both the same, they do have a common factor — low nitrogen. I find it hard to believe that fertilizers in these proportions are suitable for a leek, bearing in mind that nitrogen activates leaf growth, and that a leek is almost entirely leaf.

Many exhibitors avoid the decision by feeding an equally balanced fertilizer at all times, i.e. a ratio of 1:1:1. The leeks appear to do very well, and many win shows, but have they reached their maximum potential?

I know of at least one exhibitor who provides a 1:1:1 ratio of fertilizer and who also gives a high-nitrogen liquid feed on two occasions while the leeks are in pots. Quite clearly, leeks must have a definite requirement for nitrogen and the other components, and experimentation will ultimately show what it is.

I have been interested in this problem for some time: while a solution may appear at first to be easy, consider for a moment a fundamental difficulty. It is convenient to think in terms of high nitrogen or low nitrogen, but what if the plants first of all require a low nitrogen and subsequently a high nitrogen — and if so when should the change be made? The same difficulty arises with the other fertilizers and, as they are given with the nitrogen feeds, there are many possible permutations.

A few considerations with regard to seasonal development of the leeks may be appropriate at this point. All the fertilizers have advantages, as far as we are able to assess the true requirements of the plants. Phosphates encourage root development. During the early months of the year, when light intensity is low, it would be advantageous for the plant to develop roots and not leaves. A liquid feed in the ratio of 1:2:2 therefore would seem ideal at this time.

As the plants grow, daylight hours and light intensity also increase and the liquid feed can be changed to a ratio of 1½:1:1 to provide slightly more nitrogen. This proportion would be suitable until the leeks are planted in trenches. Alternatively, the liquid feed can be increased to one of high nitrogen, with a suggested ratio of 3:1:1; however, I personally consider this to be too high and not conducive to steady growth.

Once you decide to give leeks a liquid feed it must be done regularly. Although once a week may be recommended, why not consider feeding twice a week, with half the recommended concentration?

The permutations for the leek grower are endless and personal choice based upon experimentation over the years is going to be the deciding factor. A knowledge of the leek being raised and the judicious use of fertilizers will ultimately ensure that the potential of the leek is reached.

Foliar feeding is not an alternative to liquid feeding; the two complement each other. Foliar feeds should be regarded as growth stimulants rather than as fertilizers. Specific foliar feeds are available, but do ensure that the concentration is accurate, so that you avoid damage to the leaf surface.

While the exact mechanism is not known, the conditions that encourage the active absorption of nutrients are fairly well established. The absorption rate is higher in humid conditions: for this reason an application in the early morning or evening is preferable to one at midday. Young leaves are also more responsive than older ones: this makes it seem more sensible to use a foliar spray in the greenhouse rather than when the leeks enter their trenches.

A very fine mist spray should be used and the foliage of the leeks drenched. I like to foliar feed daily from March onwards although it has its uses before then. Regular spraying for the first week that 'grass leeks' are removed from the seed head and planted, keeps them fresh and provides nourishment until they produce roots. Secondly, foliar feeding can be used as a tonic for leeks that, for one reason or another, are not doing as well as others.

GROWING FROM SEED

Leeks raised from seed are genetically variable and, although this may make it difficult to find two or three similar leeks for the showbench, raising from seed is an excellent way of discovering new strains (see *Figure 6*).

The compost used for seed can be the same as that used for potting. However, the physical structure is more important than the fertilizer content, for the leek seedlings will be removed soon after their arrival at the surface of the compost.

I prefer to use a deep plastic seed tray of the type which usually forms the base of the cheaper propagators. A root develops first and can become quite long before the first leaf appears at the surface. Shallow trays are unsuitable because this root grows down and bends at the base. Then, when the seedling is being removed, the bent portion may break off and the seedling becomes exposed to infections.

The compost should almost fill the tray and is pressed gently down to create a space of about half an inch (12 mm). I use a block of wood for this purpose and it should be noted that there is no need to press firmly; gentle, even pressure is all that is necessary.

The small black seeds can be thinly scattered over the surface; avoid seeds coming into contact with the sides of the tray and never over-sow. More compost can now be added to the depth of the tray. After gentle firming a space of about a quarter of an inch (6 mm) will remain. The tray is placed in lukewarm water for a few minutes until the compost becomes moist at the surface; then it is removed to drain.

'Damping off' diseases are always a problem and over-watering is often the cause. As a general guide the seed tray may need watering only once more, about eight or nine days after sowing. Cheshunt compound added to the water on both occasions will help to prevent damping off. In addition the seed can be 'dressed' before sowing by mixing with a small amount of fungicidal powder in the seed packet before sowing — thiram, benomyl or captan can be used.

I prefer to cover the tray with glass to prevent excessive evaporation. Germination will take place in approximately ten days at a temperature of 16°C (61°F), but do not discard the compost until three weeks has elapsed. Some seeds are noticeably slower than others to germinate, and it is worth waiting for them; although they do not all catch up on the early germinators, some always will, and these vigorous ones are worth keeping.

The seedlings will appear in a crooked shape and as soon as they are visible the glass cover should be removed. When they are about half an inch (12 mm) high and still in a crooked shape they can be potted into 3 inch (75 mm) pots which will, of course, contain the selected growing medium and complete fertilizer.

GROWING FROM 'GRASS' LEEKS

The alternative to seed is 'grass', the name given to the miniature leeks (bulbils) which grow on the seed head of long leeks and some pot leeks (see *Figure 7*. The 'grass leeks' have been obtaining nourishment from the seed head and on removal should be planted immediately into 3 inch (75 mm) pots. Any delay will be detrimental and usually results in heavy losses.

To facilitate easier removal of the 'grass', a knife can be used to bisect the seed-head stalk about one inch (25 mm) from the head. The two halves can be gently pulled apart and the head will slowly split in two, making the 'grass' more accessible.

The potting compost should be gently firmed and a hole made in the centre about half an inch (12 mm) deep for pot leeks and 1¼ inches (30 mm) deep for long leeks. By holding the leaf, the base of the 'grass' can be positioned in the hole and the compost firmed to secure its position. The compost can then be watered using a can with a fine rose. Alternatively, the pots can be filled with dry compost and watered the previous day; this will allow excess water to drain and the temperature of the damp compost will warm to that of the greenhouse.

GROWING FROM DORMANT AND SEMI-DORMANT PODS

These are characteristic of some pot leeks but not of long leeks. Larger pods resemble small tulip bulbs, pointed at one end, larger and more rounded at the other (see *Figure 8*). Dry scale leaves cover the pods and protect them from dehydration. If they are particularly loose they can be removed but, wherever possible, should remain to protect the pods in storage.

The size of pods varies, even when the pods are from the same seed head. The largest are about three-quarters of an inch (18 mm) in diameter, with an average size of a quarter of an inch (6 mm).

Sometimes the pods are not completely dormant and the first leaf and root initials may be evident. The pods should be pushed into moist compost, one per 3 inch (75 mm) pot with the pointed end uppermost and I like to insert the pod so that the tip alone is showing. With the larger pods, water the compost only when the surface shows signs of drying. Too much water inhibits root development and the pod often decomposes.

A temperature of 10°C is adequate and, because of the large food store, development is rapid, far exceeding that of the 'grass leeks' in the initial stages. When the pod has become 'spent' it then becomes a source of infection because it decays in the area that is most vulnerable, i.e. the base of the plant; the pod should therefore be removed.

The spent pod can be removed with care as soon as the plant has developed two leaves, but do not remove the plant from the compost. The pod should be exposed by pushing some of the surface compost to one side. The pod can be split lengthways with the thumb nail and then carefully removed from the leek (see *Figure 9*). A little practice is required to develop the technique and the larger pods respond better than the very small ones. Pods under a quarter of an inch (6 mm) in diameter should not be removed for fear of damaging the leek plant with the thumb nail.

PODS OR SEED?

Pods and 'grass' are vegetative organs of perennation and will genetically resemble the parent plant. Pods from the same seed head, irrespective of size or shape, will be the same. For this reason, keep only those leeks that are of good quality and ideally those that have been exhibited: their progeny will be equally good.

Seeds are variable but well worth raising, for although some will not have desirable qualities, others may be better than the parents; these are the ones to isolate and keep for another year in order to collect their pods and produce a new variety.

Unfortunately it is not always possible to recognize desirable qualities at the seedling stage but many can be discarded after a few weeks' growth. Twisted, 'blind', very long, or diseased specimens can be discarded at an early stage. The rest may have to complete their life cycle for the first year before it can be definitely decided whether or not the plant is worth keeping.

This may appear to be a lot of trouble for a single seed, and it is, but it is only from seed that new strains of pot leek arise — a worthwhile thought, perhaps, when finding room for them in the trenches.

LEEK CLONES (STRAINS) AND THEIR SELECTION

Leeks which share identical characteristics are known as clones and are given names to distinguish them, for example the 'TL', 'Patterson' and 'Newcastle' clones. However, in general conversation between leek growers the words 'type' or 'strain' are used, rather than 'clone'.

Leeks from seed are variable and few are identical in appearance although many may share a single common characteristic. Such variation in leeks grown from seed prevents them from being classed as a distinct clone. However, by raising from seed a grower is able to produce many individual plants, some of which may have desirable qualities worthy of propagation. The qualities in the plant raised from seed are transferred to the 'daughter' plants provided that they are propagated vegetatively, i.e. from pods or 'grass'. Seed from the 'mother' plant usually produces a wide variety of seedlings with a multitude of characteristics; few, if any, will resemble the 'mother' plant.

Robinsons of Forton, near Preston, have managed to produce leek seed that gives plants that are distinctly different from others, but reasonably similar to each other. Years of selection and isolation are required to achieve this, and must be continued to maintain the qualities found in their plants.

Robinsons produce 'Mammoth' pot and long leeks. In my opinion, it is their long leeks that are much more of an exhibitor's plant, as they develop long lengths of blanch with reasonable girth. Their pot leeks, on the other hand, are modest specimens, but are perhaps ideal for smaller shows or where a 'collection of vegetables' is to be exhibited.

Sinclair McGill of Kelso, Scotland, produce long leeks and pot leeks known as 'Mayfield Column' and 'Mayfield Pot' respectively. They are new introductions and it would be unfair to comment at this stage on their potential for the exhibitor. However, I understand that the 'Mayfield Pot' can easily be grown into an intermediate leek, which should attract the exhibitors who wish to enter this new class.

The 'TL' pot leek, also referred to as the 'Hindson' pot leek, has been a top exhibitors' leek for many years. The *News of the World* leek was possibly a 'TL' although no longer referred to by leek growers. This clone is not often seen in its original form: selective breeding by various growers over many years has led to a number of variations. In addition, the incidence of leek virus has influenced the colour of the leaf and sometimes the general growth habit of the plants, as it does with all clones in time. The 'TL' characteristics are basically of upright growth, with the length of blanch often exceeding the limit for pot leeks and venturing into the intermediate class. Small 'teeth' or serrations are evident on the leaf blade and the shape of the blanch area is that of a wedge when grown to sizes above 100 cubic inches per pair; this wedge becomes more pronounced with increased size.

The 'Nine Pin' has few devotees although it is an attractive pot leek on the showbench. The plant in the trench is very upright and the new flags do not readily separate, producing a 'spire' in the centre of the plant.

The 'Patterson' pot leek is of Northumbrian origin, where the tradition was for a short length of blanch. It requires long collars to lengthen the plant in the greenhouse (see pages 50–51). The flags are wide and growth is not upright as it is in the 'TL' and 'Nine Pin' leeks. The 'Patterson' produces a fan shape in profile; the 'TL' is often referred to as palm shape. One distinguishing feature of the 'Patterson' pot leek is that a reddish-brown coloration appears on a small area of flag.

The 'TL', 'Nine Pin' and 'Patterson' are available only from leek growers and exhibitors. They are occasionally advertised for sale in the gardening Press, but meeting exhibitors at the shows is likely to be more rewarding.

'Elliot's Original' (see the *cover illustration*), named after my son, and offered by Marshalls of Wisbech, Cambridgeshire, was the best of the pot leeks raised from dormant pods. It consistently has grown to over 100 cubic inches per pair, with 120 cubic inches being close to maximum. This leek is a good 'club leek', in that it is suitable for shows at which leeks smaller than those seen at the open shows are likely to be exhibited. Leeks from dormant pods are usually coarse with thick flags; removing one often results in a great loss of circumference. However, 'Elliot's Original' had some quality and won a great many shows in the North and in the Midlands. A crop failure at Marshalls prevented its inclusion in the 1983 catalogue but this leek clone may be re-advertised for sale.

Long leeks can be grown from 'Mammoth' and 'Mayfield Column' and Suttons of Torquay also offer 'Prizetaker' which originated from the very old 'Lyon' leek. There are fewer named exhibition long leeks than pot leeks, but there are many unnamed clones being raised by amateur exhibitors who often advertise their 'grass' in the gardening Press in December and January, with young plants being available in March and April.

Exhibitors of long leeks should be sought; many will sell their surplus stock. Specimens that are straight, not bulbous, and have the ability to produce girth as well as length, are ideal for exhibiting. At some northern shows the cubic capacity of long leeks is estimated and Levi Carr of Annfield Plain, near Stanley in County Durham, holds the record of 206.6 cubic inches with his own clone of leek.

It is important that any exhibitor carefully selects the plants that are to be used for propagation and that all others should be eaten or destroyed. Vigorous selection of only the best leeks will develop and improve the clone.

Naturally, the leeks the exhibitor chooses to show will form the main stock, but two or three others from the leek trench can be kept in reserve. An exhibitor who raises many leeks for sale is not as selective, for here numbers become more important than quality. My advice when buying from leek growers is to avoid those growers that have huge or numerous greenhouses. The exhibitor with a small greenhouse has to be selective, so his plants are more likely to be of an excellent standard.

Once you have achieved a good clone of leek, try to raise it yourself and be as selective as possible. Within a few years you will have a clone that is unique. It will have characteristics of the original, but in addition there will be features that you personally have seen and, having decided that they are desirable, kept.

In 1980 I introduced a pot leek clone which I named the 'Newcastle' strain which had been selected from a seedling raised and seen as having some promise a few seasons earlier. It became the leek of the year in 1980, winning many shows and also growing to be the largest at 170 cubic inches per pair (see *Figure 10*). I have re-selected this leek and have tried to eliminate some of its faults. Already I have a clone that is slightly different and, I hope, better; I have named it the 'Newcastle Improved'.

Those who obtained the 'Newcastle' leek in 1980 will have tried to do as I have done, and it is possible that there are now a small number of newly named plants from my original clone. The qualities desirable in a leek are identical to those that the judge seeks. Size alone, without quality, is not desirable and such plants are not suitable for propagation.

Many smaller shows are spoiled by large numbers of leeks of moderate size without quality. It is the duty of a judge to penalize these plants severely and it is the desire of the exhibitor to achieve something that is better, by selective breeding.

TIMING FOR EXHIBITION

The time to sow seed and plant pods, or 'grass', is variable but late December and early January represent the peak time. Ideally, if the leek has been grown for a few years the exact timing will be known; if not, I would recommend the first week of January.

There may not seem to be much difference between the end of one month and the beginning of another; in fact there is a world of difference. Leeks have a definite period of growth, after which they will stand for a while and then begin to lose their appearance. The outer flags will soften and others will go limp, necessitating the removal of many flags before the leeks can be exhibited.

Some pot leeks have a growing period of up to nine months and, if this is taken as an example, I will illustrate how planting time is important. The best pot leeks are exhibited when still growing strongly, not the ones that reached maximum size a week before the show and have just stood still for that period of time. Consequently, with the 'nine-month' leek, a period of eight and a half months should be allowed from starting off to exhibiting them.

Decide which shows you are to enter: some can be in late August, others in early October, with the majority occupying dates in September. As an example, if you are to enter a late September show, your pot leeks should be started in mid-January for a period of eight and a half months.

Now imagine the worst: planting in late December for an early October show — a period of over nine months. In this instance the plants will have reached maximum size some three to four weeks earlier.

The growing period will vary according to how the seedlings are treated in the early part of the year. If the temperature fluctuates, or a very high temperature is maintained, then the example of nine months' growth will be upset.

Keep a record of when the leeks were started and when they were at their best. The following year try to maintain the same conditions and time the planting for particular shows.

With seeds, the timing will not be known accurately for they will not be the same as the parent plant and their growth period could be different. Seeds will keep for a few years in cool, dry conditions, although the germination expectancy will fall. Dormant pods will not keep for long periods and by March most will have started to decay. Very small pods with a growing leaf, i.e. 'grass leeks', will keep for only as long as the seed head supplies nourishment. A problem of many seed heads is that they are subject to decay; when this happens the 'grass' is also at risk.

It is possible to save the 'grass leeks' from a decaying seed head until the time of planting. The method is to remove them from the seed head in the usual manner and to plant them in boxes of damp sand about 2 inches (50 mm) apart. The aim is for the damp sand to keep them fresh without starting them into growth. Losses can be expected, but it is a method that generally works well. Place the box in a well-ventilated, semi-light position (full sun should be avoided). Maintain low but frost-free temperatures and do not allow the humidity to rise too high . The plants will not grow, of course, but by keeping them moist they will stand until planting time, when they should be carefully removed and the normal planting procedure followed.

TRANSPLANTING

As the leeks outgrow their 3 inch (75 mm) pots they must be transplanted into 5 inch (125 mm) pots. Transplanting must not be delayed or plant growth will be checked. The 5 inch (125 mm) pot should have a layer of lightly compressed compost at the base and the 3 inch (75 mm) pot should be well soaked. All is now ready for the transplanting process.

The 3 inch (75 mm) pot should be inverted with the open fingers of one hand supporting the compost. The other hand can be used to tap the base of the pot, allowing the whole compost to slide out; this can now be placed centrally in the larger pot.

Add compost to fill the gap between the root ball and the pot side; this can be firmed with the thumbs of both hands. Finally, the whole pot can be watered, drained and replaced on the greenhouse staging.

Exhibition pot leeks that remain longer in the greenhouse will need to be transplanted again into larger containers finishing off in 7–9 inch (175–225 mm) pots. These larger pots can be partly filled with old farmyard manure or with soil taken from the trench. This serves two purposes: first, it is economical, by saving on potting compost; secondly, it allows the plants to adapt to the conditions in the soil that they will soon be entering.

LENGTHENING THE LEEKS

This is where long and intermediate leeks differ from pot leeks in their cultivation. With long leeks, great length is desirable, provided that the circumference of the plant is not unnaturally thin. The blanch of the pot leek, however, must not exceed 6 inches (and at some shows 5½ inches). Some pot leeks develop this length naturally and an effort must be made not to plant them deeply which would encourage longer growth. Others will need lengthening, and this should be done in the greenhouse while the plants are in pots.

Leeks are drawn towards light and, therefore, shading the plants will cause them to lengthen in their efforts to reach the light. Collars can be made to encourage this process, their length depending on how much blanch is required. This knowledge comes only from having raised the variety of pot leek previously and being aware of its limitations, but 4½ inches is the average collar size.

The collar has to be wide enough to allow the plant to develop, but narrow enough to limit the light entering. If too much light enters the collar, the lengthening process will be inhibited. Lengthening the leek can start as soon as the plants are fairly sturdy — March is about the right time.

With long leeks the young plants should be planted more deeply at all stages of growth. Initially the 'grass' or 'bulbils' should be planted about 30 mm deep. They are planted out in mid to late April and this does not give much time for lengthening the blanch while in the greenhouse. It is important to maintain a robust plant and forcing their length in the early stages leaves them thin and weak.

Some growers gain a little more length when potting into 5 inch (125 mm) pots by planting a little deeper. This is acceptable and is the traditional method; however, I have been able to extend the blanch while maintaining robustness by using a short length of plastic damp-course material made into a cylinder 1 inch (25 mm) long. The cylinder is placed over the leek so that it just covers the 'button'. It is held in place by an elastic band secured to a thin cane pushed into the potting compost close to the leek. As the leek lengthens the cylinder is moved upwards, thus covering the 'button' once again.

The advantage of this is that the leek remains green and, consequently, robust and healthy. The process can also be monitored and, if the young plants are showing signs of becoming thinner at the expense of length, then the collars can be removed.

At planting-out time the base of the plant should be about 4 inches (100 mm) deep. No further attempt should be made to lengthen the blanch for about three weeks, to allow the plant to establish a good root system. A cylinder made from the same material can then be placed over the leek. Always allow at least one-third of the foliage to remain exposed, to prevent over-blanching and weakening the plant.

The cylinder can be replaced with a standard land drain tile (300 × 90 mm) and, as the leek lengthens, more tubes can be added. The process can continue up to the end of July, at which time the plant starts to resist lengthening and instead of an upward growth of the barrel, only the leaves become blanched.

Figure 1. The 1980 National Pot Leek Show held at the 'Alexandra', Grangetown, Sunderland (see page 14)

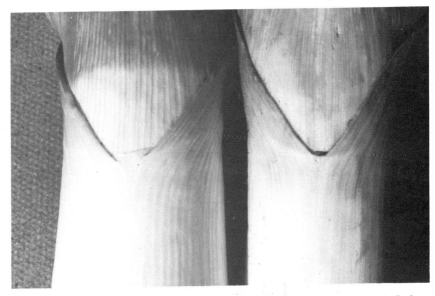

Figure 2. A leek showing a veil (left) and another (right) without a veil. Judges should be aware that the veil should be included when measuring the length of blanch in an exhibition leek (see pages 18 and 64).

Figure 3. William Mould and the 1979 'National' winners. While this was the second Pot Leek Society Show, it was the first to be called 'National'; hence he was the first 'National' winner (see page 24)

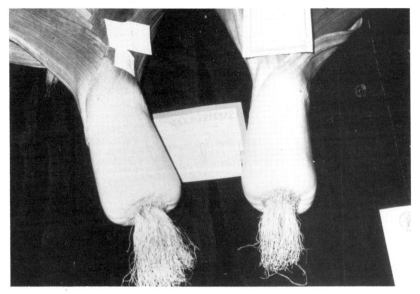

Figure 4. The largest, but second place, leeks at the 1980 National Pot Leek Show (see page 26)

Figure 5. The winning leeks at the 1980 National Pot Leek Show (see page 26)

Figure 6. Raising leeks from seed: this is the only way of achieving new varieties. Seedlings grown individually in pots tend to give better plants (see page 42)

Figure 7. A 'grass' head (see page 43)

Figure 8. Dormant pods, produced by some leeks (see page 43)

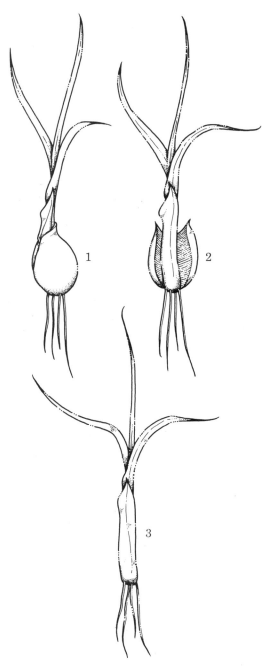

Figure 9.   Stages in removing a spent pod from a leek (see page 44)

Figure 10. A pair of pot leeks of the
'Newcastle' clone (see page 47)

Figure 11.   Soil splashed on to the 'flags' (leaves) can increase the risk of disease (see page 62)

Figure 12. Leeks for seeding are stood in a bucket containing water and a high-phosphate fertilizer (see page 65)

Figure 13. Show leeks to be kept for seeding are sometimes planted in the open ground – a method not be recommended (see page 66)

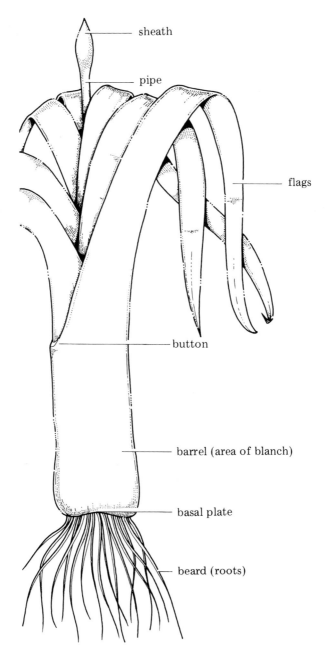

sheath

pipe

flags

button

barrel (area of blanch)

basal plate

beard (roots)

Figure 14.   A leek in its second year 'going to seed' in early June (see page 67)

Figure 15.   Stages in the development of a leek flowering head: (a) the spathe which envelops the developing head; (b) and (c) the spathe lifting off naturally; pulling this off damages the head and encourages disease; (d) the open flowers awaiting the arrival of insects to pollinate them (see page 67)

Figure 16.   A leek head full of seed (see page 67)

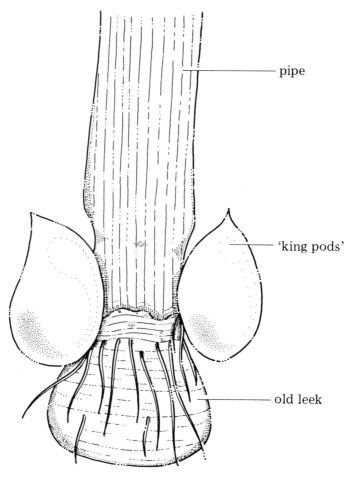

pipe

'king pods'

old leek

Figure 17.   A leek in late September, after having 'gone to seed' (see page 67)

Figure 18. 'Flags' (leaves) of a pot leek showing advanced symptoms of virus disease; symptoms are usually less apparent than this (see page 73)

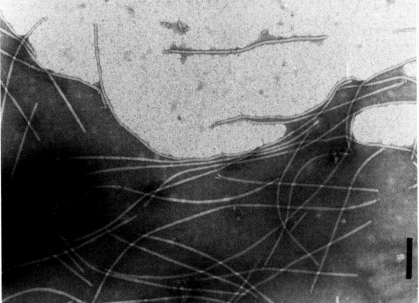

Figure 19.   Thread-like particles of leek yellow stripe virus (which causes a common disease of leeks) photographed under the electron microscope and shown here magnified many millions of times. The bar in the bottom right-hand corner represents 200 nanometres (there are one million nanometres in a millimetre!) (see page 73). MAFF Crown Copyright ©

Figure 20. A pair of pot leeks well presented for the show bench (see page 81)

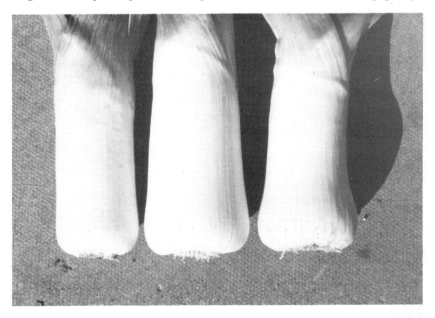

Figure 21. Parallel (left), wedge (centre) and bulbous (right) leeks. The latter are a serious fault and would be penalized by the judge (see pages 81 and 82)

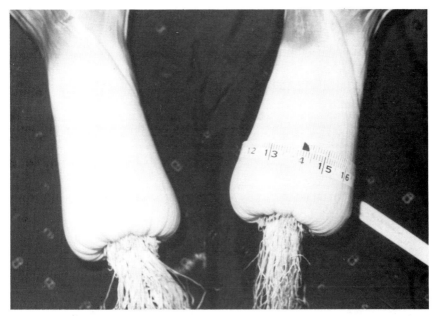

Figure 22. Measuring the circumference of a pot leek (see page 81)

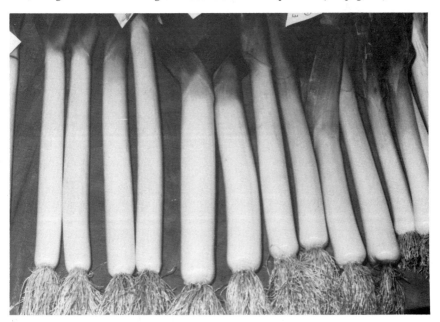

Figure 23.   Many leeks that would have been considered 'long' a few years ago would now be classified as 'intermediate' (see page 82)

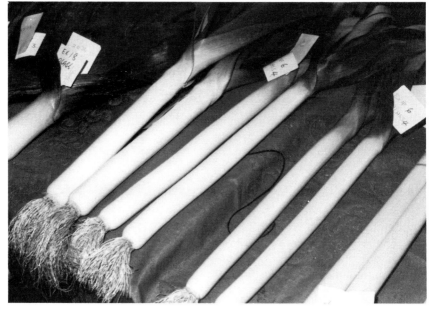

Figure 24.   'Long' leeks awaiting the judge (see page 82)

Figure 25. Alan Herbert and the world's largest recorded pair of pot leeks (see page 92)

7

Leek Cultivation – Outdoor

PREPARATION OF THE SOIL

The final planting position for leeks is usually in a prepared trench, but this will not be necessary when ordinary garden soil is particularly light and well drained. I know of a few growers who are able to raise leeks without a prepared trench. Their methods are so similar that the basic outline is worthy of inclusion here.

Cow manure is stacked for a period of one to two years, at the end of which it will be well decomposed, and slicing it with a spade will not be difficult. The manure is rotavated into the soil during the late Autumn and each square metre has up to one full barrowload of manure added; this procedure is repeated each season.

The acidity level of the soil will steadily rise with the addition of organic material. In order to stabilize this, basic slag is applied every third year at a rate of 4 oz/square yard (120 grams/square metre). Basic slag contains lime, which neutralizes acid; it is also a recognized phosphate fertilizer and this phosphate is slowly released. In spring, blood, fish and bone fertilizer is added to the surface soil at a rate of 8 oz/square yard (240 grams/square metre) and gently worked into the surface.

Most leek growers have unsuitable soil: it is therefore necessary to prepare a special site for the leeks, known as a trench. Trenches are used for season after season and, for this reason, their preparation is particularly important.

The perfect location for a trench is in full sunlight; anything less will be detrimental to plant growth. Avoid overhanging trees and shading from any buildings. Preparing the trench is hard work in most soils; give the site careful consideration, therefore, so that this laborious task need be done only once.

The trench should be positioned in an east-to-west direction so that all the available sunlight will get to all plants. Unfortunately, open sunny sites are often windy and care must be taken to avoid damage to the leek flags, which easily twist and break. Fine netting is a suitable wind break and, when secured around the leek trench, is useful insurance against high winds.

A trench can be made entirely above ground, at ground level, or slightly above ground level. Trenches of the first type often become too dry, especially if watering is done infrequently or inadequately, and are most susceptible to high winds. The trench at ground level can become a 'soak-away' in poorly drained soils; such trenches fill with water and, whereas leeks enjoy plenty of water, it must be free draining.

The ideal location is a trench that is partly raised above ground level, where moisture will be retained without becoming waterlogged. The soil should be removed to a depth of 18 inches (450 mm) and raised to a similar height using bricks or concrete blocks. Timber is unsatisfactory because it decays and harbours pests and diseases. The width of the trench is important, 2 ft (600 mm) for a single row of leeks and 4 ft (1200 mm) for a double row.

Draining is important and the first 6 inches (150 mm) should consist of ashes or similar aggregate to allow this. Straw should be scattered over the aggregate to a similar depth; this will prevent the aggregate becoming choked with fine soil particles which would inhibit drainage.

The trench becomes a site for manure to age and the resulting decomposition produces some warmth for the upper layer. In the first year the fresh manure is added to a depth of 450 mm and the trench is completed by the addition of a good soil mixture. In subsequent years the old manure will form an integral part of the soil mixture, while fresh manure will always remain at the lower level of the trench.

The soil mixture should not be taken from the garden if it was originally unsuitable for raising leeks. Topsoil passed through a 6 mm riddle and mixed with peat and riddled ashes or grit sand in the proportions 2:1:1 will form an excellent medium.

In subsequent years the soil mixture and manure are removed and mixed together allowing the addition of fresh manure to the lower level. More soil, peat and grit sand can be added, together or individually, to maintain the physical structure of the soil.

Cow manure added to the soil or prepared trench has produced the best leeks over the years. Why this is preferable to all others is not known but may be related to the way in which the animal digests its food. The nitrogen, phosphate and potash levels are low, but numerous trace elements are present. Manure adds bulk to the soil, and makes it porous (which is most important) and yet is water-retentive and, consequently, fertilizer-retentive.

Other organic materials are available for leek growers to use: these include mushroom compost, with a composition of 2% nitrogen, 1.5% phosphates and 2% potash. Seaweed abounds in trace elements and, with a typical analysis of nitrogen 1.5%, phosphates 1% and potash 5%, appears to be ideal for leeks. Unfortunately it also contains a large amount of common salt and therefore needs to be composted on the surface for a long time to reduce the salt content, although leeks are tolerant of some salt.

Spent hops will improve the physical structure of soil but is not a good manure substitute; it contains about 3% nitrogen and 1% phosphates. Sewage sludge is also useful as a soil additive, with 5% nitrogen and 6% phosphates. It contains many trace elements, but some can be in excess and are therefore damaging. The pH is also variable but is usually alkaline and ideal for balancing acid soils.

Peat is not a food but an excellent soil additive to improve the physical structure. Garden compost is excellent if available in sufficient quantity. Hay, straw, tomato and bean haulms, sawdust and 'shoddy' (wool waste), offer alternatives to be tried, but only when manure is not available.

SOIL STERILIZATION

In the first year that a site is to be used for growing leeks it should not be necessary to sterilize the soil. The exception to this is in areas where there are a great many leek growers and a preponderance of leek diseases.

The amateur grower is limited in what he can use, but the chemicals available are effective when used correctly. Dazomet is available through allotment societies, where a large pack can be divided among members. It is a white powder that is worked into the surface layer of the soil at a rate of 480 g per 5 square metres. The area must be covered with polythene and weighted down to maintain a good seal.

Warm soil conditions are needed to break down the chemical, which liberates sterilizing fumes. Late September is an ideal time to do this, when the season's leeks have been removed. The treatment can be carried out in spring, but it is essential to separate sterilizing and planting-out by a few weeks. Before planting out, remove the polythene and fork over the site to aerate the soil and release the deadly vapours.

A 5% solution of formalin is a very good alternative to drench the soil when applied at 25 litres per square metre. Polythene can be used to seal the area and an autumn application is essential. This is because formalin lasts for a long time, and a spring application would allow harmful toxins to persist, which would damage new transplants.

Jeyes fluid, when used according to the manufacturer's instructions, will also sterilize soil although I have never used it myself; however, it is readily available and offers an alternative to dazomet or formalin.

The availability of sterilizing chemicals should not give the leek grower a false sense of security. To have a 'clean' start is helpful, but it is still important to guard against pests and diseases throughout the growing period of the leek. The advice given in a later chapter on 'Diseases, Pests and Problems' (pages 69–78) should be pursued enthusiastically.

SOIL ANALYSIS, MANURES AND FERTILIZERS FOR THE TRENCH

As I have mentioned previously, the major nutrient requirements for leeks are nitrogen, phosphorus and potash, and only when an adequate supply of these nutrients is available will the plants grow to their maximum potential. Other elements are important, of course, but because they are used in small quantities and are usually always available it is unnecessary to test specifically for their presence.

Because exhibition leeks are grown on the same site year after year, the nutrients will become depleted; however, by incorporating manure and applying fertilizers, the nutrient levels can be restored. Nevertheless, only a soil analysis can reveal whether the levels have been fully restored or not.

To follow a pattern of manuring and fertilizer application each year without the guidance of a soil analysis may create an imbalance of nutrients. For example, most of the many leek trenches which have been examined revealed moderate to high nitrogen deficiencies, without a deficiency of phosphorus or potash.

An analysis will also reveal the pH of the soil on a scale ranging from 0 to 14. A pH of 7 is defined as neutral: above this, alkaline conditions exist, and below 7 the soil is acid. The pH range of soils generally is from pH 4 to pH 8 and the further the number away from 7 the more acid the soil is, i.e. soil of pH 4 is more acid than soil of pH 5.

The soil pH is very important because it controls the uptake of elements by the plant. For example, phosphorus becomes 'locked up' in the soil if the conditions are too acid, while alkaline conditions can 'lock up' manganese. The ideal pH range for leeks is 6–7.25 with the optimum being pH 6.75. Within this range all nutrients are available to the plant.

A professional soil analysis can be costly; however, savings will be made on any fertilizers that the analysis reveals are not required. There are also soil test kits available to the amateur, which will provide satisfactory results.

Nitrogen is used extensively by leeks: it is an essential ingredient of plant protein and consequently promotes growth. Leaves, in particular, benefit: they become dark green when ample nitrogen is available, whereas when there is a deficiency of nitrogen they become stunted and yellowish-green; however, this should not be confused with virus symptoms. Nitrogen is available in many materials: all organic compounds, for example, contain nitrogen, although the bulky animal manures have less than is generally assumed.

Nitrogen is quickly exhausted from the soil, although soils containing plenty of organic material retain more than light sandy soils. This element is also removed in large quantities by leaching, i.e. washing-out of the soil by rain or melting snow. It is also removed by the crops themselves and consequently this element must be replaced every year.

Phosphorus has a vital role in the general health of the leek. It promotes early growth and vigorous root formation and for this reason is added to the potting compost for leeks in the greenhouse. Without a good root system the plants will not be able to take in other nutrients in sufficient quantities, and overall size will ultimately become affected. Phosphorus is also essential to give leeks a 'winter hardiness'. Hard winters and low phosphate levels are often the cause of losing seed leeks.

Phosphorus starvation can easily occur if the pH of the soil falls and becomes more acid: liberal applications of garden compost, peat, sulphate of ammonia and/or animal manures will all lower the pH. A phosphorus deficiency is revealed by slow growth, an undeveloped root system and general ill health, possibly indicated by a bluish-purple coloration of the leaves.

Potash has many functions. It is essential for general health and growth, it aids plants to use nitrogen, and it acts as a buffer if too much lime has been applied to the soil, thereby increasing the quantity of calcium. A potash deficiency in leeks is shown by a scorched appearance of the leaf edges of the oldest leaves with a possible mottling on other areas. Growth will be inhibited and the plant will not appear healthy, nor erect.

Over one hundred leek trenches were analysed during a period from October to March. The samples came largely from the North East, but Yorkshire and Cumbria were well represented with a few samples from Scotland, Staffordshire and Northumberland. Of the samples 83.5% fell between the range pH 6–7.25, but only 15% had the optimum pH of 6.75. The highest recorded was pH 7.5 and the lowest pH 5.0.

All soil samples showed a deficiency of nitrogen and this was more evident in the early months of the year after considerable leaching by the winter rains. On a scale ranging from 'without deficiency' to 'excessive deficiency' the following results were obtained:

No deficiency	0%
Small deficiency	48%
Moderate deficiency	44%
Great deficiency	4.25%
Excessive deficiency	3.75%

Basic slag is commonly used on leek trenches to correct acidity and, as this material also provides phosphates, the phosphorus levels of most trenches was excellent. Using the same scale as above, the following results were obtained:

No deficiency	50%
Small deficiency	25%
Moderate deficiency	18%
Great deficiency	7%
Excessive deficiency	0%

Sulphate of potash is usually added to trenches as a top dressing and is also found in many proprietary fertilizers. This probably accounts for the good results obtained, which are as follows:

No deficiency	37%
Small deficiency	40%
Moderate deficiency	20%
Great deficiency	3%
Excessive deficiency	0%

The analysis of leek trenches shows the importance of getting the soil in the right condition, both chemically as well as physically. The pH and nitrogen levels show the greatest variation and should be tested at least once every year. Potash and phosphorus levels will probably remain high if basic slag and sulphate of potash are used. Proprietary top dressings contain potash and phosphorus and, when used annually, will prevent deficiencies.

A few of the leek trenches tested had very high concentrations of phosphorus and potash, which did not seem to be detrimental to the leeks. Nitrogen is the element that is most likely not to be present in the correct proportions, and one effective remedy is not to apply fertilizers in the autumn as the winter rains and thawing snow will leach the nitrogen from the ground. A spring application is much more sensible.

Slow-release nitrogen granules are available which are raked into the soil a few weeks prior to planting out, the nitrogen being released over a period of at least four months. Nevertheless, most gardeners seem to enjoy adding fertilizers and, therefore, although the slow-release granules are labour saving, they are unlikely to replace traditional fertilizer for some while.

Adding a fertilizer regularly has a number of distinct advantages. The grower knows that the plants are receiving nutrients and can adjust the programme according to the plant growth. Secondly, by applying a fertilizer it means that the plants are getting some attention: it is usually on these occasions that some problem is seen, for example, rust lesions, and therefore corrective treatment can be started immediately.

Many growers are afraid to use nitrogen, for two reasons. The first is that leeks have always been grouped with onions, for which a recommended fertilizer has been low nitrogen, high phosphate and high potash. Secondly, when a high-nitrogen feed has been used, the leeks have split deeply, confirming the general recommendation.

I believe that leeks do require nitrogen and that any deep splitting is due to the leek having reached its maximum potential, or that the nitrogen feed has been added suddenly in a desperate attempt to gain size in a short time. All feeding must be gradual, aiming for steady growth over the full growing period.

Some exhibitors maintain that if the trench is made correctly with the addition of a base fertilizer, then the leeks should receive nothing more than water to the end of the season; others start supplementary feeding immediately. Only by experimenting with your own strain of leek will you know whether supplementary feeding is necessary or beneficial. I personally believe that supplementary feeding is essential in order to achieve colossal leeks — but with which fertilizer, and how regularly it is to be applied, is a matter for experimentation once again.

A common method of applying liquid fertilizer is to use a 'feeding tube', which is a cylinder pushed at an angle towards the plant roots and down which the fertilizer is poured; short lengths of plastic downspouting or bottomless glass jars can be used for this. The disadvantages of this method are that the tube concentrates the fertilizers to one side and, as a result, root development will not be uniform. In addition, the tube acts as a wind tunnel, letting in cool air which will inhibit root growth. Finally, the soil becomes compacted at the base of the tube.

An 'advanced' feeding tube drains into a plastic plant pot: the base of the pot prevents the wind cooling the root area and the drain holes allow the liquid to flow freely, thus avoiding soil compaction. This type of tube is an improvement but, I think, is still unnecessary.

The use of 'feeder tubes' may have developed from their success with the raising of tomatoes by ring culture. The idea is that the fertilizer goes directly to the roots where it is required. This traditional method has many followers but I believe it has only disadvantages, no advantages; the majority of top exhibitors do not use 'feeder tubes'.

The following table may prove useful when selecting material for your trench or fertilizers for application to the soil. All figures are approximate, for much depends upon the age of the material and how well it has been stored. With animal manures, the composition varies according to the food eaten and because of this it is likely to be seasonal.

Table Nitrogen, phosphorus and potassium (potash) content of various materials

Material	Percentage content		
	Nitrogen (N)	Phosphorus (P)	Potassium (K)
Farmyard manure	0.5	0.15	0.4
Seaweed	1.5	0.09	5.0
Spent hops	3.0	1.0	—
Mushroom compost	2.0	1.5	2.0
Sewage sludge	5.0	6.0	trace
Shoddy	12.0–15.0	—	—
Bonemeal	2.0	25.0	—
Dried blood	7.0–14.0	—	—
Hoof and horn	12.0–14.0	—	—
Sulphate of ammonia	21.0	—	—
Nitrate of ammonia	34.0	—	—
Chilean potash nitrate	15.0	—	10.0
Nitro-chalk	20.0	—	—
Superphosphate of lime	—	18.0	—
Basic slag	—	15.0	—
Sulphate of potash	—	—	48.0
Muriate of potash	—	—	60.0

The results of a soil analysis will reveal certain deficiencies and the corrective treatment may be recommended for application in kilograms per hectare, grams per square metre, or ounces per square yard. To convert from one to the other is relatively simple. For example, to convert from kg to g divide by ten; thus 50 kg/hectare becomes 5 g/square metre. To change ounces per square yards into grams per square metre multiply by thirty; thus 4 oz/square yard becomes 120 g/square metre.

Other examples are as follows:

2 oz/sq yard	=	60 g/sq metre	=	600 kg/hectare
4 oz/sq yard	=	120 g/sq metre	=	1200 kg/hectare
6 oz/sq yard	=	180 g/sq metre	=	1800 kg/hectare
8 oz/sq yard	=	240 g/sq metre	=	2400 kg/hectare

PLANTING OUT

Leeks need to be hardened slowly to outdoor conditions before planting out. Long leeks are planted out towards the end of April and pot leeks a month later. At least three weeks should be allowed during which the plants are given protection without having artificial heat. With the pot leeks, for example, I reduce the evening temperature in the greenhouse throughout April, no heat being given in May. The use of cold frames or a polythene-clad greenhouse is necessary for the long leeks if these share accommodation with pot leeks.

Ventilators will be open at first during the day only; at the end of the month they are open all the time. Common sense must prevail at this time and if there is a cold wind blowing into the greenhouse it is best to close the ventilators on that side. Plants must be hardened slowly and with care so that there is little check to growth.

Watering the plants in pots at this stage of their development is a daily routine. Water the plants thoroughly, for greenhouse temperatures can rise very high during the day. Potting compost should never be allowed to dry out and, provided that it is free draining, no harm will come to the plant.

On the day before planting, the trench soil should be well watered and the plants given a liquid feed. On the morning of planting out, each one should be sprayed against rust, using a fungicide and incorporating a wetting agent. Later in the day the plants are removed from the greenhouse or cold frame and individually planted. A large hole must be dug to accommodate each plant; your choice of potting compost for final potting can be used to fill the hole until the correct level is reached.

A long leek will be planted so that the base of the plant is about 4 inches (100 mm) below soil level. Pot leeks should be planted to the level of the lowest button. The plants must be carefully positioned so that the tips of the flags on one side point east and those on the other side point west; in this position all the foliage receives sunlight. A north–south orientation would result in the upper leaves shading all the others.

Long leeks require a planting distance of 18 inches apart (450 mm) and pot leeks 24 inches (600 mm). The soil should never dry, but the amount of water given depends upon the local weather conditions and how well-draining the trench is; therefore the surface soil should always be dark. Watering can be done overhead; it is a myth that watering this way will damage the leeks. With a large number of plants, an overhead sprinkler can be used: the type that produces a mist spray is preferable to a lawn sprinkler, as the latter produces a much larger water droplet that often 'pans' the surface of the soil, as well as throwing soil up onto the foliage (*Figure 11*).

The water a plant takes in can be referred to as 'soil water' for it will contain substances dissolved in the water which will be the plant's food. Water flows through the soil by the pull of gravity, but some is always held back by soil particles and particularly by organic material. The 'field capacity' is the amount of water held by the soil against the pull of gravity, i.e. what remains after drainage. Sand alone will have a low field capacity, whereas the organically rich soil found in leek trenches will have a high field capacity.

As water is removed by the plants and evaporation the tension force of the water in the soil increases. Eventually this force is stronger than the ability of the plant to take in water. The leek grower must be aware of this because soil that appears moist may not be wet enough to allow the plant to absorb water. The field capacity must be maintained at all times and this means the regular application of large amounts of water.

STRIPPING THE FOLIAGE

While long leeks are producing their upward growth, pot leeks are creating girth, and their increased size causes the older, outer flags to split and then to decay. The leek exhibitor must be aware that this is happening and must remove the decaying flags.

Some growers merely pull at the decaying outer flag, causing it to snap off at soil level; this is unacceptable for it leaves the base of the flag in contact with a healthy flag. You must find time to attend to each leek every week and the soil around it must be cleared, exposing the leek down to the base; this allows the outer flag to be closely inspected.

If the flag has only just split, then it can be left for a further week. If it has split and opened extensively, it should be removed; the flag at this stage is often still green, but do not wait for it to become brown and papery. To facilitate the removal of the flag, I split it into three or four strips and pull at each one in turn, ensuring that they detach cleanly at the base.

Leaving the old flags in position to decay attracts slugs and also increases the corrugation of the leek. Ideally, the blanched area of the leek should be smooth, but a wavy, corrugated appearance develops if stripping is not done regularly.

There are other advantages of this practice: in particular, the soil is kept loose and therefore does not restrict the growth of the leek. Stones and pests can also be removed, but in a well-made trench these should not be present. The only time the outer dead flag is allowed to remain in place is the week prior to the show, because it then acts as a 'guard' to the flag beneath and is removed only on lifting for the show.

PREPARATION FOR THE SHOW

Schedules for shows will indicate whether two, three or six leeks are required. In the case of pot leeks, the schedule will also indicate the length of blanch area not to be exceeded. All measurements are to a tight button, which is one that has not split: as the button includes the veil, this must also be intact, if present (see *Figure 2*).

Carefully lift the tubes from long leeks and inspect the length of blanch and circumference so that a near-perfect set of leeks can be staged. Discrepancies in length are more obvious to a judge with long leeks than with pot leeks. With pot leeks, although the stand may appear uniform, the cubic capacity, if measured, is rarely identical.

From the first day of August to the date of the show, all pot leeks should be measured around the girth each week and the measurements recorded. This can be done when the leeks are stripped of their outer flag and, if the leeks in the trench are numbered, it makes the recording much easier.

The beginning of August is chosen because those still standing will be the leeks that are going to continue; those that have seeded, twisted, or bent over for various reasons will have been pulled up and consumed. The circumference at this time, measured around the middle of the blanch area, will be at least 8 inches, possibly 9 and sometimes 10 inches. Pot leeks less than 8 inches may still be acceptable for smaller shows and for some outside the main pot-leek regions.

The circumference will increase rapidly throughout August and into September, but this rate of increase will then begin to slow down. Leeks that do not increase in size between two consecutive measurements have reached their maturity and are past their best. Leeks starting to slow down are ready for showing, while those still forging ahead can be left for the later shows at the end of September and early October.

This knowledge of the leek can come only from measurement: it is not so easy to estimate by observation alone. If a leek has reached its maximum and appears to be in good form and the date of the show is close, then it may be saved. To leave it in the trench, even for a few days, may cause it to split uncontrollably: however, if a spade is used to lift the leek, thus breaking its roots, the plant will not split but will remain fresh. This practice is to be used only in an emergency, where a particular mature leek is needed to make up a stand of leeks of similar size. Lifting is therefore carried out in order to break the roots, but the leek must then remain in the trench.

Having selected the leeks, lift them carefully on the day before the show. Wash the soil off the roots using a hosepipe; the roots are fragile and no attempt should be made to shake or pull the soil off by hand. Do not allow the water, which will be carrying soil particles, to enter the flags, because it will be difficult to remove the soil particles from between the flags.

The guard flag should still be in place when more careful removal of soil from the root plate is done, using the hosepipe with a jet attachment. When the soil has been removed, examine the flags, trim off any ragged tips and, with fingers crossed, make sure that it is not going to seed. The judge will be feeling for the seed head and will disqualify any leeks that are going to seed.

With this completed, place the leeks on a table top protected by a damp towel. Carefully remove the guard flag and trim the root plate with a knife, removing all pieces of old, discarded flags. At this stage I grip the roots and trim them evenly; I think it makes for a much neater presentation but unfortunately it is not a common practice.

The leeks are then placed in a bucket containing clean water and are left until they are transported to the show the following day. Examine the button the following morning and, if it has split, remove the flag; if it has not yet split it will certainly remain intact for the duration of the show. Wrap the leeks separately in the damp towelling, place them on a baker's tray and transport them carefully to the show.

AFTER THE SHOW

With judging completed, the leeks will have to remain on display for two days and possibly more. The conditions are detrimental to the leeks, which deteriorate rapidly. It is very important to remove your leeks as soon as possible and to take them home to prepare them for seeding.

On arrival at home, cut off all the roots as close as possible to the root plate. This may seem drastic, but these roots are dead and, if left, will only decay around the area where the new root growth will develop. Stand the plants in a bucket to about one-third their depth in water to which a high-phosphate fertilizer has been added, and place the bucket where it is shaded and cool — the floor of a garage is ideal (see *Figure 12*).

The following day strip off the two outer flags and trim all the remaining flags so that they do not trail on the ground; do not cut the young centre flags. After a few days, and up to one week later, inspect the base of the leek. New roots should be evident and when they are seen, the leek can be planted.

A bucket is an ideal plant container but requires drain holes; add a few pieces of crock and use a sterilized potting compost to fill the container. Pot and intermediate leeks need to be planted to a depth only of half the blanch area; long leeks should be planted as deep as possible and then supported with a garden cane. Once this has been done, the potted leek can be placed in a cold greenhouse where winter losses will be minimal. No liquid feeding is required and, initially, watering should be done with care to encourage the development of the roots.

During the following season the leek can be left in the container and, if seed only is required, it should remain in the greenhouse for better pollination and ripening. If 'grass' or dormant pods are wanted, they will grow too early in the warmth of the greenhouse: the leek in its container should therefore be taken outdoors, placed in a sheltered area in April, and returned to the shelter of the greenhouse in October.

The exhibitor who raises leeks from 'grass' will benefit by this method, for the developing grass can remain on the plant until it is time to propagate from them. Until my method was developed, seed leeks were planted in a sheltered area of the garden, often with disastrous results (see *Figure 13*).

In the garden the show leeks have little time to produce roots before the soil temperature becomes too cold. As the outer flags decay, the plant becomes smaller and does not fill its planting hole: consequently, in a wind it will rock to and fro, inhibiting any further root development. Diseases are more likely to persist and pass to the new season's leeks when planted out.

The greatest problem with seed leeks planted in the garden is that a seed head with 'grass' must be cut off the plant in October and kept healthy until early January, when propagation starts. This caused exhibitors to have numerous losses. In attempts to avoid such losses, some stood the cut heads in water; others inverted the head, created a hollow in the base and poured a liquid sugar feed into it daily. The answer — to grow the seed leeks in containers — was simple enough but eluded those who relied solely on traditional methods.

THE SEEDING LEEK

The leek in its container, with the protection of a greenhouse, will survive the winter and, in early summer, a seed head will begin to show (see *Figure 14*). Growth is rapid at this stage and the 'pipe' or stem will need to be loosely tied to a garden cane for support. From mid-June to the end of August the sheath protecting the flower will split and come loose. Do not pull this off as you will thereby damage the base of the flower, which may then become infected, with the consequent loss of the head (see *Figure 15*).

The earliest to flower will be those that have been kept in a greenhouse for the whole time. Leeks in their second year will also flower early, but leeks kept over successive years by keeping the basal bulbs will flower later.

Bees, wasps, hover flies and a variety of insects will visit the flower and soon the process of pollination will be complete and a swollen green seed case will be evident at the site of each floret. There are hundreds of these on every head and each will hold three or four fertile seeds (see *Figure 16*).

If the head is being kept for seed alone, cut it off with about 6 inches (150 mm) of stem in mid-October. Hang the head upside down in a warm room and in mid-December the seed cases can be rubbed between the hands. The black seed will fall freely and can be stored in a cool, dry place.

If you want 'grass', the flower can be 'shaved' in mid-September. This involves trimming off the individual seed cases with their short stalk. Collect and store them in the warmth; the seeds will ripen and can be extracted. The shaved head meanwhile will quickly develop the young leek plants known as 'grass', which will be removed for propagation in January.

Some exhibitors trim only around the head leaving a tuft of seed to develop on the crown. I cut off all the seed cases and usually an abundance of 'grass' develops. Long leeks usually form a head of seed with 'grass' evident, and this is best left intact on the head until January, when both can be removed.

At the base of the leek plant one or two large bulb-like structures will appear to replace the old and dying plant. These will produce flags and also a seed head and this process continues indefinitely, thereby ensuring the survival of the plant; some leek growers refer to these as 'king pods' (see *Figure 17*).

8

Diseases, Pests and Problems

Magazine articles and books written by authors who do not grow leeks themselves, have put about the idea that the leek is hardy and is not susceptible to many pests and diseases. Those who actually grow leeks may never receive the accolades bestowed on these authors, but we know that such information is far from correct.

Leek rust has been prevalent in the past, and leek virus (although less noticeable to the untrained eye) is widespread. Fusarium root rot, botrytis, white tip and white rot of leeks are less common, but very troublesome when they do appear. In the greenhouse, aphids are the main pests of leeks, while slugs, soil larvae and caterpillars of the leek moth are troublesome outdoors. Other problems include wind damage, over-watering, nutrient deficiencies and a dry atmosphere. Hailstones, cats, birds, weeds and footballs are other problems encountered with monotonous regularity. Last, but not least, theft and vandalism are other problems encountered by leek growers.

DISEASES

Leek rust

Leek rust is the most common of the diseases that attack leeks. It is caused by a fungus called *Puccinia porri* and, like many other rust diseases, it tends to be specific to a few host plants. In theory, leek rust should be able to attack any member of the leek family including onions, chives and garlic. In practice the rust appears to attack leeks only, and I have even seen onions grown alongside infected leeks without detriment.

Rust reproduces by way of spores which are released into the atmosphere; because they are so light they can travel for many miles before settling. Heavy rainfall may wash them down but it is unlikely that they would then adhere to leek foliage that sheds water readily.

Light rainfall and humid conditions are more likely to be conducive to the spore's development on foliage. Leeks are under attack throughout their period of growth outdoors, although the disease is more noticeable during July and early August, particularly in a cool summer.

Orange-coloured pustules appear and initially are about the size of a pin-head. However, growth is rapid and, as more spores are released, the pustules quickly develop over much of the foliage. I have seen rust pustules occupying over 50% of the leaf area, although 5–10% is more likely.

The incidence of rust on pot leeks has been exceptionally high since the early 1970s and was at a peak around 1977. The milder winters experienced during this period would certainly have contributed to the increase. Obviously, the fungus was better able to survive; therefore colonies increased more rapidly in following years.

Following the hard winters of 1978–79 and 1981–82 the number of rust-infected plants has been reduced. The rust fungus can survive only on living tissue and, as both farmers and exhibitors lost plants, the rust problem should not be so severe for many years.

At the moment the chemical treatment for rust is limited. Mancozeb, triadimefon, or zineb, will form a protective barrier to the rust spores but these fungicides must be sprayed on to the plants before the rust appears. The first application should be carried out immediately the leeks are planted out and at fortnightly intervals thereafter. Spraying regularly is essential, particularly after heavy rain, which washes off the protective chemical. New growth will not have a fungicidal barrier and this is another reason why a regular spraying is necessary.

The foliage of leeks is naturally glossy and sheds water easily; for this reason, a wetting agent can be added to the spray. I would advise the use of a proprietary wetting agent, but a few drops of washing-up liquid will serve as a readily available alternative.

In *Amateur Gardening* in 1976 I recommended that rust-infected foliage should be removed and burned and that seed leeks should be kept as far away as possible from the current year's plants. In January 1978, at the first 'Pot Leek Symposium', Maureen Doherty, lecturing on leek rust, emphasized the same point.

Bad management has been the cause of 'rust epidemics', in addition to the mildness of the winters. Unfortunately, even today we can find infected seed leeks growing close to the current year's plants! In the mid-1970s a few exhibitors who had rust-free plants were accused of having a secret formula. The truth was, that they practised good management and, as the seed head developed, all flags were removed leaving only the stem supported by a cane. On the rare occasions that rust was present on the stem, vaseline was smeared over the pustules, thereby preventing the release of spores and thus limiting the infection.

White tip

White tip is closely related to potato blight and thrives in similar atmospheric conditions. The fungus, *Phytophthora porri*, causes a bleaching of the older leaves usually starting at the tip, which gives rise to its name. The spores can survive in the soil for many years so, after stripping the infected leaves, do not leave them on the soil to cause contamination. Regular spraying of a fungicide is important to maintain the health of leeks. Mancozeb and zineb are useful, but captofol is better and should be used from late June onwards at regular intervals. When the disease becomes noticeable, soil sterilization will be necessary at the end of the season and is most effective when the soil is still warm — September is a good time immediately after all leeks are removed. Formalin at 5% strength and used at 25 litres/square metre, or dazomet, will prove effective (see Chapter 7, page 56), but the manufacturer's instructions must be carefully followed.

Botrytis

Botrytis cinerea is better known as grey mould and has been known to attack leeks, leaving a bleached area similar to white tip. The damaged area is usually lower down the leek and it is noticeable earlier in the season. There are many fungicides for *Botrytis* but they must be used regularly in damp cool summers when this fungus becomes most active.

White rot

This fungus, known as *Sclerotium cepivorum*, is less of a problem to leeks than to onions. However, when it does attack, the results are catastrophic. Often the disease manifests itself at the seedling stage, with all the plants collapsing just above soil level. As a soil-borne disease this problem is more likely to occur if unsterilized soil has been used in the potting compost. Use Calomel dust as a precaution when planting leeks and regularly sterilize the soil where the leeks grow.

Pink rot (root rot)

This disease of leeks is caused by the fungus *Fusarium colmorum*. It is evident on the blanched area as discoloured streaks which often have a pink tinge. The fungus is soil borne and while the infection can work upwards from the roots, any soil entering the flags could carry the infection down. It is a disease that is much more common than was at first thought and is often mistakenly called 'soil marks' by leek judges.

Pink rot is largely responsible for the loss of seed leeks when these have been planted in garden soil and not in containers where sterilized potting compost is used. The base of the leek becomes very wet, slimy and malodorous and decomposition is rapid. Soil sterilization is essential, while the use of benomyl will help to protect healthy leeks.

Black rot

Black rot is also known as *Stemphylium*; this specifically attacks the leek at the seeding stage. Usually the neck just beneath the seed head is diseased and this often results in the loss of the head and consequently the stock for the next season. Stems which have been cut off and placed in water seem to suffer the most. To prevent black rot, raise seed leeks in containers, strip all foliage from the 'pipe' and spray with fungicides.

Viruses

Until 1979, viruses in leeks had not been recorded in Britain. This does not imply that they did not exist, merely that they had not been recorded. In the Netherlands a virus called leek yellow stripe had been recorded and Dr J.T. Fletcher of the Ministry of Agriculture and myself took an interest in this disease. Exhibitors were visited, shows attended and leek plants were raised at the Ministry of Agriculture, Fisheries and Food laboratories at Kenton Bar, Newcastle upon Tyne.

The virus (which some scientists believe to be more of a chemical than a living organism) is very small and able to be transmitted easily. It is spread vegetatively, i.e. by 'grass' and dormant pods, also by contact, and by insect vectors such as greenfly and thrips. Leeks raised from seed are darker and healthier because the virus is not transmitted in this way; however, they can become infected quite easily by the methods described. In addition, the use of a leek stamper by some clubs is a means of spreading the virus unless the stamper is sterilized after each leek is marked.

No leeks on the showbenches were found to be free of virus infection, which shows itself in the general paler green colour of the flag and streaky appearance when held up to the light (see *Figure 18*). High nitrogen feeds may cause the flag to darken but will not eradicate the disease. It has been suggested that the growth of leeks is inhibited by up to 20% because of the virus. It is also responsible for aberrations in the growth of some leeks, for example twisting, bending and deformed seed heads.

Some leeks seem more tolerant of the virus; these are the ones to show and keep for propagation. However, there is some logic in raising plants from seed each year, selecting and keeping the best, and raising from 'grass' the following year. By doing this the amount of virus can be reduced and it is hoped that the size of leek can be increased. Raising continually by vegetative propagation will gradually result in the demise of that particular variety of leek.

Samples of leek flags were collected from exhibitors at the 1980 National show. I gave these to Dr Fletcher and some were examined under the electron microscope at the National Vegetable Research Station. The length of the virus particles is of particular interest because it is sometimes indicative of a particular form (see *Figure 19*). In eighteen samples, three had only one form of virus present, nine had two forms, two had three forms and four had four forms. Leek yellow stripe virus and possibly shallot latent virus were present in large numbers.

During 1979 I supplied plants to Ward and Newton of Richmond in order that an attempt could be made (by an associated laboratory) to eradicate the viruses present. In 1980 J. Soulsby, A. Atkinson, A. Mills and myself formed a partnership to sell virus-free leeks. Although the idea was sound and the leeks being provided were superb, the laboratory concerned failed to do the work because of the sudden absence of their expert in that particular area and the partnership dissolved.

PESTS

Soil pests

In the main, these are the larvae of beetles which live underground in fertile soil devouring plants until they reach maturity, when they develop into the winged insect and fly or crawl away. They include cutworms, chafer grubs, wireworms and leatherjackets. Annual soil sterilization for the treatment of diseases will also eradicate these pests, but for added protection, dust a soil insecticide around the leeks at planting-out time. I believe the cutworm to be the main problem but I do not give any the chance of a free meal.

Slugs

Although leeks come low down on their list of favourite foods, slugs will attack them at any stage of their development.

No slugs should exist in any greenhouse, while outdoors good management can help reduce their population. Always be tidy, and never leave wooden seed trays, damp sacks, or plant remains on the ground; these are favoured haunts of slugs.

Pellets of methiocarb or metaldehyde scattered in a greenhouse or placed in popular slug haunts outdoors will attract and kill these pests. They dislike sand and this can be used as a barrier to protect the crop. Numerous other methods exist to trap slugs and all can be employed when a population is high. Stale beer in a can will attract and drown them, empty dome-shaped orange skins will attract them so that they can be removed, and salt will also kill them.

Aphids

Aphids, or greenfly, can be a serious problem to young leeks when in the greenhouse. They often seek shelter within the seed head during autumn and when the heads are brought indoors they multiply. 'Grass' leeks suffer in particular because the presence of a living leaf offers food for the multitudes of greenfly.

Aphids are often overlooked and as the young plants are trying to develop they are continuously weakened by these sap-sucking insects. The problem is made worse by the introduction to the greenhouse of certain plants that are renowned for greenfly infestation, e.g. chrysanthemums and fuchsias.

If a greenhouse is to be used only for leeks and the seed head is sprayed with an insecticide there should be no further problems. However, these insects are extremely adaptable and new generations develop an increased resistance to chemicals: to avoid this happening, therefore, use two insecticides and alternate their use until the problem is overcome.

Leek moth

This is more a pest of onions where the caterpillar tunnels into the hollow leaves and devours the plant. I have never seen any leeks damaged by these caterpillars but the insecticides used to control scale insects, aphids and thrips will also control the leek moth.

Thrips

These tiny insects, sometimes called 'thunder flies', suck sap and in some years can reach epidemic numbers. Leek trenches in sheltered areas and overgrown with weeds are prone to infestations whereas those in more open aspects can remain thrip-free. Thrips are vectors of leek viruses and it is important to eradicate them, particularly if leeks are being raised from seed which could be free of virus.

Scale insects

These are so named because of a protective 'shield' that covers their body. They are not often seen and recognized as insects for, when adult, they remain motionless on a leaf, sucking sap with their mouthparts.

There are various types of scale insects in numerous colours. On leeks I have seen only green ones up to 10 mm in diameter, although usually smaller. Malathion sprayed over the foliage will control them; however, if only a small number are present they can be removed physically with a brush.

Weeds

These are plentiful where the soil is rich — an obvious problem of leek trenches. Hand weeding is preferable to avoid damage to the leeks; particular weed problems are chickweed and nettles. Weeds shelter insect pests and if they are allowed to grow they will also shade the leeks and be in competition with them for food.

Cats

These will seek the best, finest soil for their latrine and rarely use their owner's garden; I hate them and most leek growers would agree with me.

The best control is to grow the leeks in fruit cages which are surrounded by netting. Protecting the trench when not in use by stretching nylon fishing line over the area will also keep them out; otherwise it is a difficult problem.

Birds

Fruit cages once again can solve the problem but otherwise it is difficult. Both cats and birds scratch in the soil and throw it into the leek flags, thus increasing disease and marking the blanched area.

MISCELLANEOUS PROBLEMS

Ball games

These are not allowed by law on the public highway; if you are troubled by balls entering the garden, exercise your rights! A fruit cage will also keep balls out, although this is an expensive method.

Wind damage

Leek flags are prone to movement and will tear, but even minor movements will cause the button to split. Protect the leeks with wind-proof netting which allows circulation but decreases velocity.

Short leeks

This is not a problem of long and intermediate leeks, where further blanching can continue until the end of July. With pot leeks the length must be gained in the greenhouse, using collars.

Long leeks

This constitutes a problem only with pot leeks and indicates the excessive or unnecessary use of collars or the loss of too many flags during the period of growth in the trench.

Bolting

Bolting is otherwise known as 'going to seed' prematurely. Technically, the leeks have had a shock to their system but isolating this is sometimes impossible. Excessive heat in the greenhouse, drying in the pots or the trench, subjection to a cold spell, inadequate 'hardening off' prior to planting out, are all possibilities.

Splitting

This occurs in a leek which has passed its maximum size prior to being shown; alternatively, a sudden feed of high-nitrogen fertilizer or a sudden application of water after the leeks have experienced a drought, can cause splitting.

Suckers

These are leek plants developing from the basal plate of the maturing plant. With long leeks, occasionally lift the blanching tubes and remove the suckers by pushing down at their bases. Pot leeks can be treated similarly; however, some suckers grow up through the flags of maturing leeks. To leave them on would mean disqualification at the show; flags must be removed in order to get at the suckers, which results in a reduction in circumference. Suckering leeks are a real problem and propagation should be with the plants that have not produced them; in this way the suckering habit will be gradually eliminated.

White tips

In the greenhouse this can be caused by contact with the glass (i.e. damage by cold), or by a dry atmosphere. Give the plants regular foliar feeds and water sprays, particularly if electric or solid-fuel heating is used. White tips on mature leeks may indicate *Phytophthora porri* (see page 71).

Yellow leaves

This is natural if the outer flag is left on for too long. If it is a problem with more than one flag and the veins remain green, it indicates a magnesium deficiency and can be caused by an excessive use of potash; prevent this by a regular soil analysis. To correct the magnesium deficiency, spray fortnightly with magnesium sulphate (Epsom salts) at 19 grams per litre. This problem is often associated with a deficiency of calcium; maintain a correct pH to avoid over-acidity. Three grams per litre of calcium chloride sprayed each fortnight will correct the deficiency.

Poor root development

This is caused by a lack of phosphates in the potting medium, overwatering or poor drainage. The biggest leeks have the best root system!

Theft and vandalism

Lack of success will enable you to avoid this problem: however, win your show once, and you will have to become more security conscious. It is not a myth that leek growers sleep on their allotments prior to the show! In 1981 the Northumbria police recommended the use of special pens that can be used to mark the leek flags; the mark is invisible until illuminated by ultraviolet light and could help to identify stolen leeks. Leek plants are very expensive to purchase and cultivate — I would like to see this factor reflected in the sentences passed on the relatively few cases that actually reach the courts.

SECTION THREE

This details the methods used to judge leeks and explains exactly how points are awarded, or lost at a show. The 'Open' leek shows of more modern times are detailed and finally a folk song and list of Northern recipes is included for those who wish to eat, rather than to exhibit, their leeks.

9

Judging

The Royal Horticultural Society have classified long and pot leeks as twenty point vegetables, the points being awarded as follows:

condition, 8;   solidity, 8;   uniformity, 4.

With leeks the condition would include aspects such as freshness, cleanliness, a healthy appearance with no blemishes, and free from disease (*Figure 20*). Solidity is an indication of how well the leeks have been grown; they should have a high density and not be soft and uncharacteristically light in weight. Uniformity includes the shape of the leek and how it compares in shape and size to the others making up the stand (*Figure 21*).

The traditional northern method recognizes these aspects but in addition the cubic capacity of the leek is measured. In general, bigger leeks take priority because of the difficulty in growing them, as it is easier to grow smaller leeks and gain perfection. Some judges view size as the most important factor and largely exclude other aspects; these are not good judges. There are also judges who do not measure accurately, so it is not surprising that there is a lot of discrepancy.

Exhibitors wish to know the cubic capacity of their leeks and I think it remiss of the RHS not to include this.

The circumference is found by putting the measuring tape firmly around the leek but not tight enough to cut into the leek. Some judges measure the circumference in three places (top, bottom and middle) and then find the average. This is unnecessary, favours bulbous leeks, and is time consuming. A single measurement around the middle is most fair and has been adopted by most judges.

To locate the centre a soft felt-tip pen is used to mark the leek at a point exactly midway between the button and the base. The tape is placed around the leek with its upper edge just touching the centre mark (*Figure 22*).

Measuring a leek may appear to be very straightforward but it demands a fair amount of practice to become acquainted with all the different shapes. One feature which is commonly found is an irregularly shaped base; for example, a slight prominence or hollow in direct line with the button can cause an inaccurate measurement of length. Generally, the measuring tool is held in a direct line between the button and base but to be fair with irregular leeks a slight move at the base to left or right is permissible.

If the cubic capacity of intermediate or long leeks is desired the measuring tape must be used instead of the measuring tool to determine length.

In a stand of two leeks both are measured and the cubic capacity is found for each by cross referencing the length and circumference on the tables (see pages 103–110). One leek, for example, could be 57.77 cubic inches and the other 54.91, making a total of 112.68 cubic inches.

The judge usually has an assistant and as the judge calls out the measurements the assistant finds the cubic capacity on the tables. Accuracy on behalf of both is very important but mistakes can be made by the best. In 1980 at the Stormont Main Club, Wrekenton, the leeks in first place were measured by Mr E. Raydon, who is an extremely good judge. The sizes recorded were 5.5 inches (length) × 14 inches (circumference) and 5.9 inches × 13.5 inches; the respective cubic capacities were 85.78 and 84.12 cubic inches. However, the assistant misread the Tables, for leeks 5.9 inches × 13.5 inches are 85.57 cubic inches and the total stand should then have been 171.35 cubic inches. These were the biggest leeks exhibited in 1980 and it is a little unfortunate that their true size is not shown in the records or, for that matter, on the cup!

Once the stand has been measured the difficult task of judging begins. Naturally this applies only to the stands which have not been disqualified and pot leeks found to be too long or seeding leeks will be rejected. The judge has a very responsible position; his decision to mark a card 'not to schedule' may cost the exhibitor a year's work and hundreds of pounds in prize money.

I firmly believe that it is the responsibility of the judge to show where points have been deducted and to include the reasons for the deductions. At the moment, points are synonymous with cubic inches in order to establish the position of an exhibitor. For example, a stand measuring 103 cubic inches with three point deductions would be ahead of a stand of 106 cubic inches with seven point deductions.

With pot and intermediate leeks the judge must consider the limitations to length; with long leeks there is no limit (see *Figures 23* and *24*). All leeks should be free of a bulbous base and should be as near parallel as possible (see *Figure 21*). Some of the larger pot leeks are wedge shaped but this should not be considered a great fault as with a bulbous leek. The base of the leek should be round and not oval, and free of the corrugations which reflect a fault in cultivation.

Consideration must be given to the green area of leek and not just the area below the button. Leeks with rust should not be allowed on the showbench as this is an entirely preventable disease.

Finally, I believe that the roots of exhibited leeks should be cut off to prevent them being entered in another show. Some exhibitors manage to enter two shows by stripping a flag off the leek, thus refreshing its appearance. Although the roots do darken and become brittle with age, it is not a feature that is always evident, particularly if one show follows another.

10

Leeks and Leek Shows of Modern Times

Although all types of leeks are exhibited, it is the pot leek that has the greatest number of followers. These enthusiasts are not necessarily all exhibitors — indeed they may not even grow leeks at all. However, they all participate in attending the annual leek shows which start in late August and continue through to early October. Hundreds of shows are held during this period of great activity; the exhibitors have to decide how many shows to enter, the judges have usually been booked months in advance, while the spectator must choose which shows to attend.

The shows which are going to benefit everyone are those that attract the best exhibitors and, to do so, the prize money has to be high, or the show prestigious. Under normal circumstances the top exhibitors do not like to compete with each other. They are satisfied by winning a few shows in their own locality which ensures a ready market for leek plants in the following year. These exhibitors are also able to further boost their annual 'leek earnings' by judging a few local shows. A successful and enterprising leek grower, exhibitor and judge, can afford not to work. I know of a small number of these who live quite comfortably on their leek earnings.

In 1980 a judge would receive around £100 for judging a large show; a head of 'grass' could exchange hands for a similar figure, and a dozen plants in 3 inch pots for between £25 and £50. Raising two to three thousand leeks for sale is not uncommon and expenses are often kept to a minimum; for example, some growers use vending cups, not plant pots, and those living near the Durham coastline collect sea coal to fire their greenhouse boilers. Overheads are kept to a minimum and prices kept as high as the market will stand.

Other vegetables, as well as chrysanthemums and dahlias, are also raised to maintain an all-year-round market. Some growers also keep hens for their eggs, depending upon the land they have available; therefore any large garden can become a very productive nursery. Naturally, these premises are not advertised and the owners keep a low profile. Your visit to a 'nursery' is usually by invitation and guard dogs or geese give advance warning of strangers!

I have visited most of these 'nurseries' and learned a lot from the entrepreneurs, who incidentally are often characters in their own right. I should point out that knowledge of leek growing is not usually gained from what is said, but by keeping an alert eye and an open mind. The conversation is often intentionally misleading and perpetuates the many myths of leek growing.

The shows are an essential ingredient in the business of leek sales and while top exhibitors do not like to compete against each other, to do so and win is very prestigious and paramount to good business. A prestigious show, or a show offering good prize money, will attract all the top exhibitors and these shows are called 'open' because membership of a club is not essential.

Sponsors are often attracted to these shows because of the publicity they receive, both locally and nationally. The *News of the World* first sponsored pot leek shows in the North East in 1929 and continued to do so until 1967 with a short interlude during the Second World War. This was possibly the most prestigious show of all and even now *News of the World* leeks are occasionally advertised for sale.

Information on those *News of the World* shows is very difficult to find. Local newspapers did not report on the shows, presumably because sponsorship was with a rival group. The *News of the World* itself saw the event as being important locally but, being a national paper, rarely gave the shows any coverage. Those still living who were involved with the show, and could provide information, seem to be unwilling to do so.

The *News of the World* sponsored two shows, one in Northumberland and the other in Durham. The Durham event was certainly the best and was first held in the Criterion Hotel in Durham City, later moving to the Town Hall in Market Square. The first show took place on Saturday 12 October 1929, and there were 46 entries. The winners were as follows:

G. Maughan	139.9 cubic inches
J. Alexander	140.8 cubic inches
J. Carr	149.4 cubic inches

There is no mention of the number of leeks exhibited but reported shows in later years were for three leeks and I assume that these were also for three.

The judge was obviously looking for quality, with the larger leeks relegated to second and third places.

The *News of the World* cup stood over two feet tall and was solid silver; replicas were much smaller but were also solid silver. Mr E. Raydon told me that the cup was contained in a wooden box which had a single carrying handle. The total weight of this was sufficient to cut into the hands of the toughest of manual workers by the time they had reached home. E. Raydon would have known this, having made the journey three times in 1962, 1965 and 1966 with results as follows:

    1962   172 cubic inches/three leeks
    1965   201 cubic inches/three leeks
    1966   234 cubic inches/three leeks

He is the only person to have won the event three times and was unlucky not to have won again in 1967.

In 1966 the first place prize money was £30 and a silver replica of the cup. E. Raydon wanted three replicas, one for each son, and this he achieved. I am informed that this show had a great atmosphere when held in the Town Hall. It was a three-day show and the exhibits had to stand overnight before judging began. Other vegetables and flowers were also exhibited, but the pot leeks were of prime importance.

At the *News of the World* shows the Lord Mayor of Durham presented the cup to the winner and a television personality was often present. A long queue developed outside and, as no-one wanted to leave once inside, a queue always seemed to be present. The atmosphere within was like being in church; it was quiet and visitors spoke in a whisper.

In 1962, Nancy Spain of the *News of the World* reported on the show stating that: 'The whole of one wall of Durham Town Hall was a mass of leeks, lying fat and white and green side by side giving off the unmistakable (and to me beautiful) leek smell, reminiscent of a thousand stews, soups and leek puddings of the past. The rest of the hall glowed with dahlias, chrysanthemums as well as artistic arrangements and herbaceous border flowers.'

The Northumberland event, as far as I am able to ascertain, started in Newcastle upon Tyne at the Crow's Nest public house, later moving to Bainbridge Hall and finally to the Memorial Hall at Wallsend. Three leeks were staged and L. Mossman won the event in 1961 and 1965 with 170.55 amd 231.03 cubic inches respectively. I believe the last show was won by Clark of Haltwhistle with 175 cubic inches.

Mr G. Allan of New Silksworth holds the *News of the World* record with 239.31 cubic inches for three leeks in 1950. The County show was also won by him in 1950 with two leeks measuring 139.9 cubic inches, beating the pair with which he won (132 cubic inches) in 1948 at the Durham County Workingmen's Club annual show. These wins established him locally as a premier leek grower; even today his name is mentioned when leek growers become nostalgic over a pint at the local public house.

Leeks that consistently win shows are often given a name and become eagerly sought after. Initially they are only available from the original exhibitor but within a year or two other growers are able to propagate and sell the same clone. Unfortunately some are unscrupulous and (perhaps inadvertently) sell leeks of that name when they are, in fact, entirely different. In addition, a clone will change over the years, leading to a similar, but distinctly different, type of leek. The Mossman leek offered today in some areas of Northumberland, and any *News of the World* leeks, will not be identical to those originally exhibited.

Where individual growers concentrate upon a particular clone and ruthlessly eliminate all that do not show the distinguishing features, the clone will still change but may have more features in common with the original form. The Patterson leek with its faint red tinge on the flags has remained reasonably true to form. The Nine Pin leek is also very much like the original, both being available from a very limited source.

The 'TL' leek is the most well known, having won the majority of 'open' shows since the last war. Regrettably, it is rarely seen in its original form because it is grown by so many, each with their own slightly different clone. While named after Tommy Lowen its first appearance was pre-war and T. Lowen obtained it only after 1945. T. Hindson won the Delves Lane club show with this leek measuring 116 cubic inches/pair just after the 1939–45 was and a few growers still call the leek the 'Hindson' leek.

The Bass leek show started in 1973 and ended in 1980; the sponsors were Bass North East of brewery fame. The event was held each year at the Bay Hotel in Whitburn just north of Sunderland. Two leeks comprised a stand with a 6 inch length of blanch permitted. Chrysanthemums, dahlias and other vegetables were also exhibited, but the queue outside largely represented those wanting to see the pot leeks. Entry was made even more difficult by the revolving doors and once inside, no-one wanted to leave.

This was certainly a premier show and I am partly responsible for its demise (as I shall explain below), but the main damage was done by the bad publicity resulting from the judging of the 1979 show. Leek growers, exhibitors and spectators alike could not comprehend how the judge had taken 25 points off a pair of leeks, thus pushing them into second place. Throughout the following months the Bass show and the judging were discussed whenever leek growers met.

The pressure on a judge in these situations is tremendous; it compares with that of a referee awarding a penalty between two football teams on a local Derby — half the spectators agree with him and the other half do not. Unfortunately, with leeks it is usually only the winner and his friends who agree with the judge and everyone else finds fault with the judging. In reporting the show in 1979 I wrote that 'The final decision is that of the judge, but everyone is entitled to their opinion and many felt that he was wrong, irrespective of what judging system he used. Clearly, the need for a universal system is long overdue so that all exhibitors and enthusiasts will have no doubts about how points are deducted.'

My part in the demise of the Bass leek show was that I organized the National show on the same weekend: the National attracted 86 exhibitors compared with 52 at the Bass show. In 1980 the Bass show was held for the last time: the show was brought forward one week to avoid competition but the result was the same — total disaster! Thirty-four prizes were available but only 31 exhibitors bothered to enter, despite a first prize of £200. The hotel did not stay open for the full period, there were no queues and the atmosphere was like a football game with one team missing!

The official reason for the cancellation of the Bass leek show was given as increasing competition and high prize money in the area. However, the flower, vegetable and leek show sponsored by the *Evening Chronicle* was established only two years before the Bass show and still exists despite £25 first place prize money in 1980. Sponsorships are readily available just as long as the advertising remains good. Immediately there is some ill feeling between organizers, exhibitors and sponsors, then the latter withdraw. Most 'open' shows in my experience end this way but 'officially' this is never mentioned.

The results for the Bass shows are as follows:

1973	G. Stonehouse	120.9 cubic inches/pair
1974	Mr Graves	136.4 cubic inches/pair
1975	J. Jones	154.7 cubic inches/pair
1976	M. Murray	149.12 cubic inches/pair
1977	C. Marr	131.9 cubic inches/pair
1978	J. Clark	120.73 cubic inches/pair
1979	G. Stonehouse	123.34 (2nd D. Cooper 148.2)
1980	J. Davison	137.8 cubic inches/pair

The *Evening Chronicle* show is held each year at the Civic Centre in Newcastle upon Tyne. Three pot leeks are required and the maximum length of blanch is 6 inches. It was first held in 1971 and as it is organized by the Newcastle and District Horticultural Society its future appears to be secure. Pot leeks do not dominate the event; there are impressive displays of chrysanthemums, dahlias and other flowers and vegetables. However, the pot leek class offers the highest prize money (£50 for 1st in 1983) and is responsible for attracting visitors to the show.

In 1979 the Sanderson 'Top Leek Championship and Flower Show' was founded. The sponsors, Sanderson's of Morpeth, are wine and spirit merchants in the North East. The competition was held over four days at the North of England Equestrian Centre, Morpeth in Northumberland. The first prize was £1000 which was the highest awarded in a leek class at that time, with generous sums of £400 and £200 for second and third places. Lucrative cash prizes, trophies and other awards made this event well known in the North East and elsewhere in the gardening world.

It was a prestige event and was initially formed to repay a debt for the support given to Sandersons by local clubs and public houses. Four years later the show collapsed; apparently it was felt that, commercially, the wine and spirit merchants were not benefiting from the event. It is of interest to note that the reasons for cancelling the show are conflicting with the reasons for establishing the event in the first place! However, this is business and I am sure that sponsored events all end the same way sooner or later.

According to a report in *Garden News*, Sandersons also believed that too many prizes were falling into the hands of too few exhibitors, thereby ruining the contest. This is certainly evident in most leek shows where large monetary sums are awarded. The simplest form of deceit is for a good leek grower to enter the show in his own name and to use a friend to enter another stand on his behalf. Any prize money awarded is shared, of course, but the prestige of winning always goes to the leek grower because his best leeks are entered under his own name. To avert suspicion the associate in this crime is also a fellow leek grower. A few years ago it was suggested that a 'ring' of leek growers existed solely for the purpose of accumulating prizes and prize money. The best clones of leek were not widely distributed and therefore other leek growers were denied the opportunity of ever winning a big show. The formation of the National Pot Leek Society and nationwide distribution of my own leeks helped to diminish, but not to eliminate, this monopoly.

The Sanderson show was also unique in having the length of blanch limited to 5¾ inches; this was to accommodate both traditional Northumbrian and Durham exhibitors. In Northumberland 5½ inches was the accepted length while in Durham shows were 6 inches. 'Open' shows are always 6 inches, putting the Northumbrian exhibitor at some disadvantage. The Sanderson show provided a compromise which was novel, even if unnecessary. The majority of leek shows are now 6 inches and the top exhibitors, even those in Northumberland, raise their leeks with this in mind. The results for the Sanderson shows are as follows:

1979	J. Howard	145.85 cubic inches/pair
1980	J. Wilkinson	132.5 cubic inches/pair
1981	A. Henderson	155.5 cubic inches/pair
1982	J. Jones	153.9 cubic inches/pair

In 1980 the Kestrel Lager British Open Leek Championship was established and was held in Ashington, Northumberland. Three leeks with a maximum blanch length of 6 inches were required to make a stand. This event also included a 'world' onion competition which, as things turned out, saved the day for the leek show. The organizer had hoped the leeks, in addition to the onions, would also be a 'world' event; however, entries for the leek event were very small and all came from within a day's drive of Ashington! Nevertheless a record onion did appear and this made the headlines, ensuring the show's success when it so nearly was a disaster.

The event was held again in 1981 and its survival was ensured by the winner, F. Bell, creating a new record for three leeks. They measured 245.02 cubic inches, beating the long-established 1950 record of G. Allan with 239 cubic inches in the *News of the World* show. The prize money of £1200 for first place, and the lack of competition as a result of the collapse of the Bass event and demise of the National, helped to make this a good show.

In 1982 a new record for three leeks was established with a stand of 263.90 cubic inches by R. Bell. However, they were placed second by the judge, just as the record-breaking leeks of 282.7 cubic inches grown by T. Thompson were in 1983. The 42 cubic inch difference between T. Thompson's leeks in 1983 and the winning trio created discontentment in the leek fraternity similar to that surrounding the 1979 Bass show. I can only repeat, how difficult it is to be a judge!

The show at Ashington holds the record for the most changes in its title, both officially and unofficially. Once the 'British Open', then 'British and European' and now 'World Open' and yet I understand that the organizer still awaits a single entry from beyond the Northern Counties! It is regrettable that sponsors are so eager to make their show the biggest and best that they overlook other factors which, eventually, cause their shows to founder. The conditions of entry, the prize money and the judging are three areas that require careful scrutiny.

The results for the 'Ashington' shows are as follows:

1980	J. Davidson	215.78 cubic inches/three
1981	F. Bell	245.02 (new record)
1982	J. Jones	245.70 (2nd R. Bell 263.90 and new record)
1983	J. Jones	240.24 (2nd T. Thompson 282.7 and new record)
1984	G.B. Stephenson	235.29 cubic inches

The year 1983 also saw the rise of yet another sponsored show, the Vaux Leek, Flower and Vegetable show, which requires two leeks with a 6 inch maximum length of blanch. The winner was J. Jones with 153.9 cubic inches who received prize money of £500; the show was held in Darlington. In 1984 this show was won by G. Hall with 171.96 cubic inches.

The records for three leeks have been mentioned but records also exist for two leeks as well as a record for the heaviest single pot leek. In 1969 G. Stonehouse held the record for two pot leeks, with 168.58 cubic inches. In 1975 J. Jones took this record with a pair measuring 171.19 cubic inches, only to lose it within days to G. Stonehouse who produced a pair of 172.6 cubic inches. In 1977 N. Hughes had a pair measuring 180.15 cubic inches and in 1979 A. Herbert won his show at Perkinsville, County Durham with a pair measuring 194.3 cubic inches (*Figure 25*). Unconfirmed reports suggest that this record has been broken in 1984.

The 200 cubic inch per pair pot leeks have yet to be exhibited; this measurement represents the equivalent of the four minute mile. Single leeks have been raised to over 100 cubic inches, but they are exceptional. R. Bell held the record for one leek with 100.39 cubic inches in 1977 and then bettered it in 1982 with 107.88 cubic inches with one leek from his record trio. This 1982 pot leek also held the record for weight at 9lb 7⅞ oz until 1983 when R. Hankey raised a leek of 9lb 9⅛ oz.

The Pot Leek Society show, known as the National (see page 24) developed from 1978 and is still in existence although it perhaps has never recaptured the prestige of the 1980 show, which remains the largest pot leek show ever staged, with 196 entrants. The following year, under new leadership, the show included a class for long leeks, which added extra interest to the event. Unfortunately the show was to be known as the Chempak Pot Leek Championship. This general sponsor had been used by myself previously but I had always resisted the use of the product name in the title of the show: this was because I believe a National show should set standards, as it did in 1980, without appearing to be heavily dependent upon a single sponsor.

In 1982 Chempak were once again the major financial sponsors but for the last time, although they continued to give support to the show in 1983. A class for intermediate leeks was introduced in 1982 and now with classes for pot, long and intermediate leeks the pattern is complete for others to follow. Sponsorship for 1983 finally arrived from the Peterlee Development Corporation offering support provided, of course, that the event was held in Peterlee New Town.

The results for the National shows are as follows:

1978	A. Murray	111.9 cubic inches/pair
1979	W. Mould	146.7 cubic inches/pair
1980	A. Waite	146.57 cubic inches/pair
1981	E. Brown	153.70 cubic inches/pair
	A. Murray	122.6 (long leeks)
1982	G. Stonehouse	145.61 cubic inches/pair
	R. Winlow	128.6 (long leeks)
	J. Wardrop	127.08 (intermediate leeks)
1983	J. Jones	154.7 cubic inches/pair
	A. Murray	166.85 (intermediate leeks)
	W. Wilson	126.31 (long leeks)
1984	A. Murray	152.44 cubic inches/pair
	A. Murray	148.87 (intermediate leeks)
	G. Stonehouse	113.32 (long leeks)

In the future I believe that leek growing and exhibiting will become as popular nation-wide as it is now in the Northern counties. The developments that have taken place since 1978 certainly confirm this belief. I would also predict that the 200 cubic inch measurement for a pair of pot leeks will be reached and that, with a greater knowledge of pests and diseases, a higher standard of quality will be seen on the showbenches.

The intermediate leek, I am sure, will gain in popularity and the traditional Northumberland measurement of 5½ inches for pot leeks will disappear, completely superseded by the 6 inch Durham measurement. Metrication will not arrive for at least two generations and tradition, even then, may encourage growers to use Imperial units.

To protect leek exhibitors and sponsors a common method of judging will have to be agreed. Unfortunately, the Royal Horticultural Society has delayed this agreement by further confusing the judging issue. In 1981 they introduced their point system for pot leeks which does not include a measurement in cubic inches and is not accepted.

Sponsors will still be available for leek shows and prize money will continue to be high as it always has been. In late Victorian times the highest paid skilled worker at a colliery would earn around five shillings a shift; many shows offered this and often much more. The prestige of winning, of course, is incalculable. In 1983 only the 'Open' shows offered first prizes of between £500 and £1200; club shows are usually much more modest. It is not possible to compare effectively the purchasing value of prize money from early leek shows with those of today; however, the cost in 1900 of the following items may be of interest.

1 upright grand piano, burr walnut, ivory keys	£40
1 gent's cycle	£17 17s (£17.85p)
1 sewing machine	£8
1 pair of best blankets	24s (£1.20p)
20 cwt best household coal	20s 6d (£1.02½p)
1 umbrella	15s (75p)
1 leather handbag	4s (20p)
1 bottle whiskey	3s 6d (17½p)
1 bottle London gin	2s 6d (12½p)
1 newspaper	1d (½p)

More specifically, for gardeners:

1 solid fuel boiler and pipes	£4
1 7 × 5 ft greenhouse and staging	£2 16s (£2.80p)
50 evergreen and flowering shrubs	6s 6d (32½p)
12 dahlias	4s (20p)
1 bale of peat	3s 6d (17½p)
12 potted fuchsias	2s (10p)
1 packet of seeds	2d (1p)

Recipes

The most famous recipe involving leeks is that for Cock-a-Leekie Soup, which can be found in many cookery books. These Northern recipes do not include the weights for each item used. The ingredients, apart from the leeks, are subject to local availability and individual preferences.

Beef and Leek Pie

Wash, slice and gently boil the leeks. Stew lean beef and then fill a pie dish with alternate layers of leeks and beef. Cover with gravy and put on a pie crust which can be decorated with 'pastry leeks'. Place in a moderately hot oven until the pastry is cooked.

Leek Flan

Wash, slice and boil the leeks in salted water, then simmer for five minutes. Wash, drain and cool them. Lightly bake a pastry case and add the leek together with chopped lightly fried bacon and cheese. Mix one egg with some milk and pour this over the filling. Return the flan to a moderately hot oven until golden brown (about 20 minutes). Use only the white of the leek for this recipe to avoid a bitter taste.

Leek Soup

Grate a carrot, onion and potato into a saucepan; add chopped leek, celery and cabbage. Cover with meat stock, bring to the boil and simmer for about one hour. Sprinkle grated cheese over each serving.

Canny Leek

@...verse 5 slow

shattered and lay strewn all a — round. So. . .

original faster tempo

if you're really wise you will watch your prize — Hold your

spoken...

gob and never speak — al though it's quite a freak and by it's

sung...

like a mountain peak! — and guard your can – ny leek.

He grows a canny leek
That is something of a freak
    And already it's a foot from the ground.
They say he makes it grow
With an awful secret brew
    And he waters it with Newcastle Brown.
I shouldna be surprised
If he gains first prize
    For to hear that feller speak
    He grows a canny leek.

The sewage farm supplied
Him manure on the side
 And he strengthened it with cold stewed tea,
And so it graaed and graaed
Inch by inch up to a yard
 And got thicker than the trunk of a tree.
From Crook to Pity Me
Folks'ud come to see
 For to hear that feller speak
 He grows a canny leek.

He held it with such pride
That his wife she couldna bide
 It and said he's ganning right off his head.
He nursed it day and night
Till she even thought she might
 Find it lying there aside her in bed;
And so she lay in bed
Full of fear and dread
 For to hear that feller speak
 He grows a canny leek.

He grows a canny leek
That gets bigger every week
 And he grows it in his own ba–ack yard,
But at the dead of night
Thoughts are dark and knives are bright
 So a feller better stand on his guard.
It only takes a slash
For a rude, raw gash
 And through one man's jealous streak —
 Forget your canny leek!

You should have seen his face
When he looked around the place
    And his leeks were lying slashed on the ground.
How could he tell his mates
All his hopes and aspirations
    Were shattered and lay strewn all around?
So if you're really wise
You will watch your prize —
    Hold your gob and never speak —
    Although it's quite a freak
    And by, it's like a mountain peak! —
    And guard your canny leek.

Peter Hawkins

Bibliography

Books

Class, Culture and Community (1982). W. Williamson. Routledge & Kegan Paul, London.

Man, Environment and Disease in Britain (1972). G.M. Howe. David & Charles, Newton Abbot. (Also published by Pelican Books, 1976)

Royal Horticultural Society Show Handbook (1981). RHS.

The Vegetable Garden (1885). W. Robinson. John Murray Press, London.

The Wild Flowers of Britain and Northern Europe (1974). R. Fitter, A. Fitter and M. Blamey. Collins, London.

Magazine articles and scientific papers

Leek Diseases, a socio-economic problem: J.T. Fletcher. *Open Conference of Advisory Plant Pathologists, Malvern 6–8 February 1979 (PP/O/494)*

Leek Yellow Stripe Virus: L. Bos, N. Huijberts, H. Huttinga and D.A. Maat. *Netherlands Journal of Plant Pathology (1978)* **84**, 185–204

The Leek – its history & cultivation: H. Fraser. *Gardeners Chronicle Gardening Illustrated*, 25 November 1961

The Origins of Vegetables: G. MacFarlane. *Amateur Gardening*, 8 January 1972

The following newspapers are also a rich source of material regarding past leek shows:

Durham Advertiser
Durham Chronicle
Echo, Sunderland
News of the World

The Calderbank Standards — Tables of Leek Measurements

The Tables set out in the next pages are designed to enable the cubic capacity of a leek to be ascertained quickly and accurately, once the length and circumference of the leek have been measured (in inches and tenths of an inch). In order to eliminate human error, a mathematical formula has been fed into a computer to derive the figures for cubic capacity for any given length and circumference. To use these Tables, first look along the row of figures corresponding to the length of the leek (e.g. for a 5.0 inch long leek that would be the row starting 3.58, 3.82 on page 104 and continuing on the subsequent pages, to finish with the figures 112.30, 113.64, on page 110). Then find the column of figures relating to the circumference of the leek (e.g. for a 4.6 inch circumference that would be the column on page 104 starting 5.05, 5.22 and finishing 10.10). Then the number at the intersection of the row for length and the column for circumference is the cubic capacity in cubic inches of that leek (e.g. in the example just given, 8.42 cubic inches). Similarly, a leek 5.4 inches long and with a circumference of 15.1 inches has a cubic capacity of 97.98 cubic inches.

LENGTH (inches)	CIRCUMFERENCE (inches)																			
	3.0	3.1	3.2	3.3	3.4	3.5	3.6	3.7	3.8	3.9	4.0	4.1	4.2	4.3	4.4	4.5	4.6	4.7	4.8	4.9
3.0	2.15	2.29	2.44	2.60	2.76	2.92	3.09	3.27	3.45	3.63	3.82	4.01	4.21	4.41	4.62	4.83	5.05	5.27	5.50	5.73
3.1	2.22	2.37	2.53	2.69	2.85	3.02	3.20	3.38	3.56	3.75	3.95	4.15	4.35	4.56	4.78	5.00	5.22	5.45	5.68	5.92
3.2	2.29	2.45	2.61	2.77	2.94	3.12	3.30	3.49	3.68	3.87	4.07	4.28	4.49	4.71	4.93	5.16	5.39	5.63	5.87	6.11
3.3	2.36	2.52	2.59	2.86	3.04	3.22	3.40	3.60	3.79	3.99	4.20	4.41	4.63	4.86	5.08	5.32	5.56	5.80	6.05	6.31
3.4	2.44	2.60	2.77	2.95	3.13	3.31	3.51	3.70	3.91	4.12	4.33	4.55	4.77	5.00	5.24	5.48	5.73	5.98	6.23	6.50
3.5	2.51	2.68	2.85	3.03	3.22	3.41	3.61	3.81	4.02	4.24	4.46	4.68	4.91	5.15	5.39	5.64	5.89	6.15	6.42	6.69
3.6	2.58	2.75	2.93	3.12	3.31	3.51	3.71	3.92	4.14	4.36	4.58	4.82	5.05	5.30	5.55	5.80	6.06	6.33	6.60	6.88
3.7	2.65	2.83	3.02	3.21	3.40	3.61	3.82	4.03	4.25	4.48	4.71	4.95	5.19	5.44	5.70	5.96	6.23	6.50	6.78	7.07
3.8	2.72	2.91	3.10	3.29	3.50	3.70	3.92	4.14	4.37	4.60	4.84	5.08	5.33	5.59	5.85	6.12	6.40	6.68	6.97	7.26
3.9	2.79	2.98	3.18	3.38	3.59	3.80	4.02	4.25	4.48	4.72	4.97	5.22	5.47	5.74	6.01	6.28	6.57	6.86	7.15	7.45
4.0	2.86	3.06	3.26	3.47	3.68	3.90	4.13	4.36	4.60	4.84	5.09	5.35	5.61	5.89	6.16	6.45	6.74	7.03	7.33	7.64
4.1	2.94	3.14	3.34	3.55	3.77	4.00	4.23	4.47	4.71	4.96	5.22	5.48	5.76	6.03	6.32	6.61	6.90	7.21	7.52	7.83
4.2	3.01	3.21	3.42	3.64	3.86	4.09	4.33	4.58	4.83	5.08	5.35	5.62	5.90	6.18	6.47	6.77	7.07	7.38	7.70	8.02
4.3	3.08	3.29	3.50	3.73	3.96	4.19	4.43	4.68	4.94	5.20	5.47	5.75	6.04	6.33	6.62	6.93	7.24	7.56	7.88	8.22
4.4	3.15	3.36	3.59	3.81	4.05	4.29	4.54	4.79	5.06	5.33	5.60	5.89	6.18	6.47	6.78	7.09	7.41	7.73	8.07	8.41
4.5	3.22	3.44	3.67	3.90	4.14	4.39	4.64	4.90	5.17	5.45	5.73	6.02	6.32	6.62	6.93	7.25	7.58	7.91	8.25	8.60
4.6	3.29	3.52	3.75	3.99	4.23	4.48	4.74	5.01	5.29	5.57	5.86	6.15	6.46	6.77	7.09	7.41	7.75	8.09	8.43	8.79
4.7	3.37	3.59	3.83	4.07	4.32	4.58	4.85	5.12	5.40	5.69	5.98	6.29	6.60	6.92	7.24	7.57	7.91	8.26	8.62	8.98
4.8	3.44	3.67	3.91	4.16	4.42	4.68	4.95	5.23	5.52	5.81	6.11	6.42	6.74	7.06	7.39	7.73	8.08	8.44	8.80	9.17
4.9	3.51	3.75	3.99	4.25	4.51	4.78	5.05	5.34	5.63	5.93	6.24	6.55	6.88	7.21	7.55	7.90	8.25	8.61	8.98	9.36
5.0	3.58	3.82	4.07	4.33	4.60	4.87	5.16	5.45	5.75	6.05	6.37	6.69	7.02	7.36	7.70	8.06	8.42	8.79	9.17	9.55
5.1	3.65	3.90	4.16	4.42	4.69	4.97	5.26	5.56	5.86	6.17	6.49	6.82	7.16	7.50	7.86	8.22	8.59	8.97	9.35	9.74
5.2	3.72	3.98	4.24	4.51	4.78	5.07	5.36	5.66	5.98	6.29	6.62	6.96	7.30	7.65	8.01	8.38	8.76	9.14	9.53	9.94
5.3	3.80	4.05	4.32	4.59	4.88	5.17	5.47	5.77	6.09	6.41	6.75	7.09	7.44	7.80	8.17	8.54	8.92	9.32	9.72	10.13
5.4	3.87	4.13	4.40	4.68	4.97	5.26	5.57	5.88	6.21	6.54	6.88	7.22	7.58	7.95	8.32	8.70	9.09	9.49	9.90	10.32
5.5	3.94	4.21	4.48	4.77	5.06	5.36	5.67	5.99	6.32	6.66	7.00	7.36	7.72	8.09	8.47	8.86	9.26	9.67	10.08	10.51
5.6	4.01	4.28	4.56	4.85	5.15	5.46	5.78	6.10	6.43	6.78	7.13	7.49	7.86	8.24	8.63	9.02	9.43	9.84	10.27	10.70
5.7	4.08	4.36	4.64	4.94	5.24	5.56	5.88	6.21	6.55	6.90	7.26	7.62	8.00	8.39	8.78	9.19	9.60	10.02	10.45	10.89
5.8	4.15	4.44	4.73	5.03	5.34	5.65	5.98	6.32	6.66	7.02	7.38	7.76	8.14	8.53	8.94	9.35	9.77	10.20	10.63	11.08
5.9	4.23	4.51	4.81	5.11	5.43	5.75	6.08	6.43	6.78	7.14	7.51	7.89	8.28	8.68	9.09	9.51	9.93	10.37	10.82	11.27
6.0	4.30	4.59	4.89	5.20	5.52	5.85	6.19	6.54	6.89	7.26	7.64	8.03	8.42	8.83	9.24	9.67	10.10	10.55	11.00	11.46

LENGTH (inches)	CIRCUMFERENCE (inches)																			
	5.0	5.1	5.2	5.3	5.4	5.5	5.6	5.7	5.8	5.9	6.0	6.1	6.2	6.3	6.4	6.5	6.6	6.7	6.8	6.9
3.0	5.97	6.21	6.46	6.71	6.96	7.22	7.49	7.76	8.03	8.31	8.59	8.88	9.18	9.48	9.78	10.09	10.40	10.72	11.04	11.37
3.1	6.17	6.42	6.67	6.93	7.19	7.46	7.74	8.01	8.30	8.59	8.88	9.18	9.48	9.79	10.10	10.42	10.75	11.07	11.41	11.74
3.2	6.37	6.62	6.89	7.15	7.43	7.70	7.99	8.27	8.57	8.86	9.17	9.48	9.79	10.11	10.43	10.76	11.09	11.43	11.77	12.12
3.3	6.57	6.83	7.10	7.38	7.66	7.94	8.24	8.53	8.83	9.14	9.45	9.77	10.09	10.42	10.76	11.10	11.44	11.79	12.14	12.50
3.4	6.76	7.04	7.32	7.60	7.89	8.18	8.48	8.79	9.10	9.42	9.74	10.07	10.40	10.74	11.08	11.43	11.79	12.15	12.51	12.88
3.5	6.96	7.24	7.53	7.82	8.12	8.43	8.73	9.05	9.37	9.70	10.03	10.36	10.71	11.05	11.41	11.77	12.13	12.50	12.88	13.26
3.6	7.16	7.45	7.75	8.05	8.35	8.67	8.98	9.31	9.64	9.97	10.31	10.66	11.01	11.37	11.73	12.10	12.48	12.86	13.25	13.64
3.7	7.36	7.66	7.96	8.27	8.59	8.91	9.23	9.57	9.90	10.25	10.60	10.96	11.32	11.69	12.06	12.44	12.83	13.22	13.61	14.02
3.8	7.56	7.87	8.18	8.49	8.82	9.15	9.48	9.82	10.17	10.53	10.89	11.25	11.62	12.00	12.39	12.78	13.17	13.57	13.98	14.40
3.9	7.76	8.07	8.39	8.72	9.05	9.39	9.73	10.08	10.44	10.80	11.17	11.55	11.93	12.32	12.71	13.11	13.52	13.93	14.35	14.78
4.0	7.96	8.28	8.61	8.94	9.28	9.63	9.98	10.34	10.71	11.08	11.46	11.84	12.24	12.63	13.04	13.45	13.87	14.29	14.72	15.15
4.1	8.16	8.49	8.82	9.16	9.51	9.87	10.23	10.60	10.98	11.36	11.75	12.14	12.54	12.95	13.36	13.78	14.21	14.65	15.09	15.53
4.2	8.36	8.69	9.04	9.39	9.75	10.11	10.48	10.86	11.24	11.63	12.03	12.44	12.85	13.27	13.69	14.12	14.56	15.00	15.45	15.91
4.3	8.55	8.90	9.25	9.61	9.98	10.35	10.73	11.12	11.51	11.91	12.32	12.73	13.15	13.58	14.02	14.46	14.91	15.36	15.82	16.29
4.4	8.75	9.11	9.47	9.84	10.21	10.59	10.98	11.38	11.78	12.19	12.61	13.03	13.46	13.90	14.34	14.79	15.25	15.72	16.19	16.67
4.5	8.95	9.31	9.68	10.06	10.44	10.83	11.23	11.63	12.05	12.47	12.89	13.32	13.77	14.21	14.67	15.13	15.60	16.08	16.56	17.05
4.6	9.15	9.52	9.90	10.28	10.67	11.07	11.48	11.89	12.31	12.74	13.18	13.62	14.07	14.53	14.99	15.47	15.95	16.43	16.93	17.43
4.7	9.35	9.73	10.11	10.51	10.91	11.31	11.73	12.15	12.58	13.02	13.46	13.92	14.38	14.84	15.32	15.80	16.29	16.79	17.29	17.81
4.8	9.55	9.94	10.33	10.73	11.14	11.55	11.98	12.41	12.85	13.30	13.75	14.21	14.68	15.16	15.65	16.14	16.64	17.15	17.66	18.19
4.9	9.75	10.14	10.54	10.95	11.37	11.80	12.23	12.67	13.12	13.57	14.04	14.51	14.99	15.48	15.97	16.47	16.99	17.50	18.03	18.56
5.0	9.95	10.35	10.76	11.18	11.60	12.04	12.48	12.93	13.38	13.85	14.32	14.81	15.29	15.79	16.30	16.81	17.33	17.86	18.40	18.94
5.1	10.15	10.56	10.97	11.40	11.83	12.28	12.73	13.19	13.65	14.13	14.61	15.10	15.60	16.11	16.62	17.15	17.68	18.22	18.77	19.32
5.2	10.35	10.76	11.19	11.62	12.07	12.52	12.98	13.44	13.92	14.40	14.90	15.40	15.91	16.42	16.95	17.48	18.03	18.58	19.13	19.70
5.3	10.54	10.97	11.40	11.85	12.30	12.76	13.23	13.70	14.19	14.68	15.18	15.69	16.21	16.74	17.28	17.82	18.37	18.93	19.50	20.08
5.4	10.74	11.18	11.62	12.07	12.53	13.00	13.48	13.96	14.46	14.96	15.47	15.99	16.52	17.06	17.60	18.16	18.72	19.29	19.87	20.46
5.5	10.94	11.38	11.83	12.29	12.76	13.24	13.73	14.22	14.72	15.24	15.76	16.29	16.82	17.37	17.93	18.49	19.07	19.65	20.24	20.84
5.6	11.14	11.59	12.05	12.52	12.99	13.48	13.98	14.48	14.99	15.51	16.04	16.58	17.13	17.69	18.25	18.83	19.41	20.00	20.61	21.22
5.7	11.34	11.80	12.27	12.74	13.23	13.72	14.22	14.74	15.26	15.79	16.33	16.88	17.44	18.00	18.58	19.16	19.76	20.36	20.97	21.60
5.8	11.54	12.00	12.48	12.96	13.46	13.96	14.47	15.00	15.53	16.07	16.62	17.17	17.74	18.32	18.91	19.50	20.11	20.72	21.34	21.97
5.9	11.74	12.21	12.70	13.19	13.69	14.20	14.72	15.25	15.79	16.34	16.90	17.47	18.05	18.63	19.23	19.84	20.45	21.08	21.71	22.35
6.0	11.94	12.42	12.91	13.41	13.92	14.44	14.97	15.51	16.06	16.62	17.19	17.77	18.35	18.95	19.56	20.17	20.80	21.43	22.08	22.73

106

LENGTH (inches)	CIRCUMFERENCE (inches)																			
	7.0	7.1	7.2	7.3	7.4	7.5	7.6	7.7	7.8	7.9	8.0	8.1	8.2	8.3	8.4	8.5	8.6	8.7	8.8	8.9
3.0	11.70	12.03	12.38	12.72	13.07	13.43	13.79	14.15	14.52	14.90	15.28	15.66	16.05	16.45	16.84	17.25	17.66	18.07	18.49	18.91
3.1	12.09	12.44	12.79	13.15	13.51	13.88	14.25	14.63	15.01	15.40	15.79	16.19	16.59	16.99	17.41	17.82	18.25	18.67	19.10	19.54
3.2	12.48	12.84	13.20	13.57	13.94	14.32	14.71	15.10	15.49	15.89	16.30	16.71	17.12	17.54	17.97	18.40	18.83	19.27	19.72	20.17
3.3	12.87	13.24	13.61	13.99	14.38	14.77	15.17	15.57	15.98	16.39	16.81	17.23	17.66	18.09	18.53	18.97	19.42	19.88	20.34	20.80
3.4	13.26	13.64	14.03	14.42	14.82	15.22	15.63	16.04	16.46	16.89	17.32	17.75	18.19	18.64	19.09	19.55	20.01	20.48	20.95	21.43
3.5	13.65	14.04	14.44	14.84	15.25	15.67	16.09	16.51	16.95	17.38	17.83	18.27	18.73	19.19	19.65	20.12	20.60	21.08	21.57	22.06
3.6	14.04	14.44	14.85	15.27	15.69	16.11	16.55	16.99	17.43	17.88	18.33	18.80	19.26	19.74	20.21	20.70	21.19	21.68	22.18	22.69
3.7	14.43	14.84	15.26	15.69	16.12	16.56	17.01	17.46	17.91	18.38	18.84	19.32	19.80	20.28	20.78	21.27	21.78	22.29	22.80	23.32
3.8	14.82	15.24	15.68	16.11	16.56	17.01	17.47	17.93	18.40	18.87	19.35	19.84	20.33	20.83	21.34	21.85	22.37	22.89	23.42	23.95
3.9	15.21	15.64	16.09	16.54	16.99	17.46	17.93	18.40	18.88	19.37	19.86	20.36	20.87	21.38	21.90	22.42	22.95	23.49	24.03	24.58
4.0	15.60	16.05	16.50	16.96	17.43	17.90	18.39	18.87	19.37	19.87	20.37	20.88	21.40	21.93	22.46	23.00	23.54	24.09	24.65	25.21
4.1	15.99	16.45	16.91	17.39	17.87	18.35	18.85	19.34	19.85	20.36	20.88	21.41	21.94	22.48	23.02	23.57	24.13	24.70	25.27	25.84
4.2	16.38	16.85	17.33	17.81	18.30	18.80	19.30	19.82	20.33	20.86	21.39	21.93	22.47	23.02	23.58	24.15	24.72	25.30	25.88	26.47
4.3	16.77	17.25	17.74	18.23	18.74	19.25	19.76	20.29	20.82	21.36	21.90	22.45	23.02	23.57	24.14	24.72	25.31	25.90	26.50	27.10
4.4	17.16	17.65	18.15	18.66	19.17	19.70	20.22	20.76	21.30	21.85	22.41	22.97	23.54	24.12	24.71	25.30	25.90	26.50	27.11	27.73
4.5	17.55	18.05	18.56	19.08	19.61	20.14	20.68	21.23	21.79	22.35	22.92	23.49	24.08	24.67	25.27	25.87	26.49	27.10	27.73	28.37
4.6	17.94	18.45	18.98	19.51	20.05	20.59	21.14	21.70	22.27	22.85	23.43	24.02	24.61	25.22	25.83	26.45	27.07	27.71	28.35	29.00
4.7	18.33	18.85	19.39	19.93	20.48	21.04	21.60	22.18	22.76	23.34	23.94	24.54	25.15	25.77	26.39	27.02	27.66	28.31	28.96	29.63
4.8	18.72	19.26	19.80	20.36	20.92	21.49	22.06	22.65	23.24	23.84	24.45	25.06	25.68	26.31	26.95	27.60	28.25	28.91	29.58	30.26
4.9	19.11	19.66	20.21	20.78	21.35	21.93	22.52	23.12	23.72	24.34	24.96	25.58	26.22	26.86	27.51	28.17	28.84	29.51	30.20	30.89
5.0	19.50	20.06	20.63	21.20	21.79	22.38	22.98	23.59	24.21	24.83	25.46	26.11	26.75	27.41	28.07	28.75	29.43	30.12	30.81	31.52
5,1	19.89	20.46	21.04	21.63	22.22	22.83	23.44	24.06	24.69	25.33	25.97	26.63	27.29	27.96	28.64	29.32	30.02	30.72	31.43	32.15
5.2	20.28	20.86	21.45	22.05	22.66	23.28	23.90	24.53	25.18	25.86	26.48	27.15	27.82	28.51	29.20	29.90	30.60	31.32	32.04	32.78
5.3	20.67	21.26	21.86	22.48	23.10	23.72	24.36	25.01	25.66	26.32	26.99	27.67	28.36	29.06	29.76	30.47	31.19	31.92	32.66	33.41
5.4	21.06	21.66	22.28	22.90	23.53	24.17	24.82	25.48	26.14	26.82	27.50	28.19	28.89	29.60	30.32	31.05	31.78	32.53	33.28	34.04
5.5	21.45	22.06	22.69	23.32	23.97	24.62	25.28	25.95	26.63	27.32	28.01	28.72	29.43	30.15	30.88	31.62	32.37	33.13	33.89	34.67
5.6	21.84	22.46	23.10	23.75	24.40	25.07	25.74	26.42	27.11	27.81	28.52	29.24	29.96	30.70	31.44	32.20	32.96	33.73	34.51	35.30
5.7	22.23	22.87	23.51	24.17	24.84	25.51	26.20	26.89	27.60	28.31	29.03	29.76	30.50	31.25	32.01	32.77	33.55	34.33	35.13	35.93
5.8	22.62	23.27	23.93	24.60	25.27	25.96	26.66	27.37	28.08	28.81	29.54	30.28	31.03	31.80	32.57	33.35	34.14	34.93	35.74	36.56
5.9	23.01	23.67	24.34	25.02	25.71	26.41	27.12	27.84	28.56	29.30	30.05	30.80	31.57	32.34	33.13	33.92	34.72	35.54	36.36	37.19
6.0	23.40	24.07	24.75	25.44	26.15	26.86	27.58	28.31	29.05	29.80	30.56	31.33	32.10	32.89	33.69	34.50	35.31	36.14	36.97	37.82

LENGTH (inches) / CIRCUMFERENCE (inches)

LENGTH	9.0	9.1	9.2	9.3	9.4	9.5	9.6	9.7	9.8	9.9	10.0	10.1	10.2	10.3	10.4	10.5	10.6	10.7	10.8	10.9
3.0	19.34	19.77	20.21	20.65	21.09	21.55	22.00	22.46	22.93	23.40	23.87	24.35	24.84	25.33	25.82	26.32	26.82	27.33	27.85	28.36
3.1	19.98	20.43	20.88	21.34	21.80	22.26	22.73	23.21	23.69	24.18	24.67	25.16	25.67	26.17	26.68	27.20	27.72	28.24	28.77	29.31
3.2	20.63	21.09	21.55	22.02	22.50	22.98	23.47	23.96	24.46	24.96	25.46	25.98	26.49	27.02	27.54	28.07	28.61	29.15	29.70	30.25
3.3	21.27	21.75	22.23	22.71	23.20	23.70	24.20	24.71	25.22	25.74	26.26	26.79	27.32	27.86	28.40	28.95	29.51	30.07	30.63	31.20
3.4	21.92	22.41	22.90	23.40	23.91	24.42	24.94	25.46	25.98	26.52	27.06	27.60	28.15	28.70	29.26	29.83	30.40	30.98	31.56	32.15
3.5	22.56	23.06	23.57	24.09	24.61	25.14	25.67	26.21	26.75	27.30	27.85	28.41	28.98	29.55	30.12	30.71	31.29	31.89	32.49	33.09
3.6	23.20	23.72	24.25	24.78	25.31	25.85	26.40	26.95	27.51	28.08	28.65	29.22	29.81	30.39	30.99	31.58	32.19	32.80	33.41	34.04
3.7	23.85	24.38	24.92	25.47	26.02	26.57	27.14	27.70	28.28	28.86	29.44	30.04	30.63	31.24	31.85	32.46	33.08	33.71	34.34	34.98
3.8	24.49	25.04	25.59	26.15	26.72	27.29	27.87	28.45	29.04	29.64	30.24	30.85	31.46	32.08	32.71	33.34	33.98	34.62	35.27	35.93
3.9	25.14	25.70	26.27	26.84	27.42	28.01	28.60	29.20	29.81	30.42	31.04	31.66	32.29	32.93	33.57	34.22	34.87	35.53	36.20	36.87
4.0	25.78	26.36	26.94	27.53	28.13	28.73	29.34	29.95	30.57	31.20	31.83	32.47	33.12	33.77	34.43	35.09	35.77	36.44	37.13	37.82
4.1	26.43	27.02	27.62	28.22	28.83	29.45	30.07	30.70	31.33	31.98	32.63	33.28	33.94	34.61	35.29	35.97	36.66	37.35	38.06	38.76
4.2	27.07	27.68	28.29	28.91	29.53	30.16	30.80	31.45	32.10	32.76	33.42	34.09	34.77	35.46	36.15	36.85	37.55	38.27	38.98	39.71
4.3	27.72	28.34	28.96	29.60	30.24	30.88	31.54	32.20	32.86	33.54	34.22	34.91	35.60	36.30	37.01	37.73	38.45	39.18	39.91	40.65
4.4	28.36	29.00	29.64	30.28	30.94	31.60	32.27	32.94	33.63	34.32	35.01	35.72	36.43	37.15	37.87	38.60	39.34	40.09	40.84	41.60
4.5	29.01	29.65	30.31	30.97	31.64	32.32	33.00	33.69	34.39	35.10	35.81	36.53	37.26	37.99	38.73	39.48	40.24	41.00	41.77	42.55
4.6	29.65	30.31	30.98	31.66	32.34	33.04	33.74	34.44	35.16	35.88	36.61	37.34	38.08	38.83	39.59	40.36	41.13	41.91	42.70	43.49
4.7	30.30	30.97	31.66	32.35	33.05	33.75	34.47	35.19	35.92	36.66	37.40	38.15	38.91	39.68	40.45	41.24	42.02	42.82	43.63	44.44
4.8	30.94	31.63	32.33	33.04	33.75	34.47	35.20	35.94	36.68	37.44	38.20	38.97	39.74	40.52	41.31	42.11	42.92	43.73	44.55	45.38
4.9	31.58	32.29	33.00	33.73	34.45	35.19	35.94	36.69	37.45	38.22	38.99	39.78	40.57	41.37	42.17	42.99	43.81	44.64	45.48	46.33
5.0	32.23	32.95	33.68	34.41	35.16	35.91	36.67	37.44	38.21	39.00	39.79	40.59	41.40	42.21	43.04	43.87	44.71	45.55	46.41	47.27
5.1	32.87	33.61	34.35	35.10	35.86	36.63	37.40	38.19	38.98	39.78	40.58	41.40	42.22	43.06	43.90	44.74	45.62	46.47	47.34	48.22
5.2	33.52	34.27	35.02	35.79	36.56	37.35	38.14	38.93	39.74	40.56	41.38	42.21	43.05	43.90	44.76	45.62	46.49	47.38	48.27	49.16
5.3	34.16	34.93	35.70	36.48	37.27	38.06	38.87	39.68	40.51	41.34	42.18	43.02	43.88	44.74	45.62	46.50	47.39	48.29	49.19	50.11
5.4	34.81	35.59	36.37	37.17	37.97	38.78	39.60	40.43	41.27	42.12	42.97	43.84	44.71	45.59	46.48	47.38	48.28	49.20	50.12	51.05
5.5	35.45	36.24	37.04	37.85	38.67	39.50	40.34	41.18	42.03	42.90	43.77	44.65	45.54	46.43	47.34	48.25	49.18	50.11	51.05	52.00
5.6	36.10	36.90	37.72	38.54	39.38	40.22	41.07	41.93	42.80	43.68	44.56	45.46	46.36	47.28	48.20	49.13	50.07	51.02	51.98	52.95
5.7	36.74	37.56	38.39	39.23	40.08	40.94	41.80	42.68	43.56	44.46	45.36	46.27	47.19	48.12	49.06	50.01	50.97	51.93	52.91	53.89
5.8	37.39	38.22	39.07	39.92	40.78	41.65	42.54	43.43	44.33	45.24	46.16	47.08	48.02	48.97	49.92	50.89	51.86	52.84	53.84	54.84
5.9	38.03	38.88	39.74	40.61	41.49	42.37	43.27	44.18	45.09	46.02	46.95	47.89	48.85	49.81	50.78	51.76	52.75	53.75	54.76	55.78
6.0	38.67	39.54	40.41	41.30	42.19	43.09	44.00	44.92	45.86	46.80	47.75	48.71	49.68	50.65	51.64	52.64	53.65	54.67	55.69	56.73

LENGTH (inches)	CIRCUMFERENCE (inches)																			
	11.0	11.1	11.2	11.3	11.4	11.5	11.6	11.7	11.8	11.9	12.0	12.1	12.2	12.3	12.4	12.5	12.6	12.7	12.8	12.9
3.0	28.89	29.41	29.95	30.48	31.03	31.57	32.12	32.68	33.24	33.81	34.38	34.95	35.53	36.12	36.71	37.30	37.90	38.51	39.11	39.73
3.1	29.85	30.39	30.94	31.50	32.06	32.62	33.19	33.77	34.35	34.93	35.52	36.12	36.72	37.32	37.93	38.55	39.16	39.79	40.42	41.05
3.2	30.81	31.38	31.94	32.52	33.09	33.68	34.27	34.86	35.46	36.06	36.67	37.28	37.90	38.53	39.15	39.79	40.43	41.07	41.72	42.38
3.3	31.78	32.36	32.94	33.53	34.13	34.73	35.34	35.95	36.57	37.19	37.82	38.45	39.09	39.73	40.38	41.03	41.69	42.36	43.03	43.70
3.4	32.74	33.34	33.94	34.55	35.16	35.78	36.41	37.04	37.67	38.31	38.96	39.61	40.27	40.93	41.60	42.28	42.95	43.64	44.33	45.02
3.5	33.70	34.32	34.94	35.56	36.20	36.83	37.48	38.13	38.78	39.44	40.11	40.78	41.46	42.14	42.83	43.52	44.22	44.92	45.63	46.35
3.6	34.66	35.30	35.94	36.58	37.23	37.89	38.55	39.22	39.89	40.57	41.25	41.94	42.64	43.34	44.05	44.76	45.48	46.21	46.94	47.67
3.7	35.63	36.28	36.93	37.60	38.27	38.94	39.62	40.31	41.00	41.70	42.40	43.11	43.82	44.55	45.27	46.01	46.74	47.49	48.24	49.00
3.8	36.59	37.26	37.93	38.61	39.30	39.99	40.69	41.39	42.11	42.82	43.54	44.27	45.01	45.75	46.50	47.25	48.01	48.77	49.54	50.32
3.9	37.55	38.24	38.93	39.63	40.33	41.04	41.76	42.48	43.21	43.95	44.69	45.44	46.19	46.95	47.72	48.49	49.27	50.06	50.85	51.65
4.0	38.52	39.22	39.93	40.65	41.37	42.10	42.83	43.57	44.32	45.08	45.84	46.60	47.38	48.16	48.94	49.74	50.53	51.34	52.15	52.97
4.1	39.48	40.20	40.93	41.66	42.40	43.15	43.90	44.66	45.43	46.20	46.98	47.77	48.56	49.36	50.17	50.98	51.80	52.62	53.46	54.29
4.2	40.44	41.18	41.93	42.68	43.44	44.20	44.97	45.75	46.54	47.33	48.13	48.93	49.75	50.57	51.39	52.22	53.06	53.91	54.76	55.62
4.3	41.40	42.16	42.92	43.69	44.47	45.25	46.04	46.84	47.65	48.46	49.27	50.10	50.93	51.77	52.61	53.47	54.33	55.19	56.06	56.94
4.4	42.37	43.14	43.92	44.71	45.50	46.31	47.12	47.93	48.75	49.58	50.42	51.26	52.12	52.97	53.84	54.71	55.59	56.47	57.37	58.27
4.5	43.33	44.12	44.92	45.73	46.54	47.36	48.19	49.02	49.86	50.71	51.57	52.43	53.30	54.18	55.06	55.95	56.85	57.76	58.67	59.59
4.6	44.29	45.10	45.92	46.74	47.57	48.41	49.26	50.11	50.97	51.84	52.71	53.59	54.48	55.38	56.28	57.20	58.12	59.04	59.97	60.92
4.7	45.26	46.08	46.92	47.76	48.61	49.46	50.33	51.20	52.08	52.96	53.86	54.76	55.67	56.58	57.51	58.44	59.38	60.32	61.28	62.24
4.8	46.22	47.06	47.91	48.77	49.64	50.52	51.40	52.29	53.19	54.09	55.00	55.92	56.85	57.79	58.73	59.68	60.64	61.61	62.58	63.56
4.9	47.18	48.04	48.91	49.79	50.68	51.57	52.47	53.38	54.29	55.22	56.15	57.09	58.04	58.99	59.96	60.93	61.91	62.89	63.89	64.89
5.0	48.14	49.02	49.91	50.81	51.71	52.62	53.54	54.47	55.40	56.34	57.30	58.25	59.22	60.20	61.18	62.17	63.17	64.18	65.19	66.21
5.1	49.11	50.00	50.91	51.82	52.74	53.67	54.61	55.56	56.51	57.47	58.44	59.42	60.41	61.40	62.40	63.41	64.43	65.46	66.49	67.54
5.2	50.07	50.98	51.91	52.84	53.78	54.73	55.68	56.65	57.62	58.60	59.59	60.58	61.59	62.60	63.63	64.66	65.70	66.74	67.80	68.86
5.3	51.03	51.97	52.91	53.85	54.81	55.78	56.75	57.73	58.73	59.73	60.73	61.75	62.77	63.81	64.85	65.90	66.96	68.03	69.10	70.19
5.4	52.00	52.95	53.90	54.87	55.85	56.83	57.82	58.82	59.83	60.85	61.88	62.92	63.96	65.01	66.07	67.14	68.22	69.31	70.41	71.51
5.5	52.96	53.93	54.90	55.89	56.88	57.88	58.89	59.91	60.94	61.98	63.03	64.08	65.14	66.22	67.30	68.39	69.49	70.59	71.71	72.83
5.6	53.92	54.91	55.90	56.90	57.91	58.94	59.96	61.00	62.05	63.11	64.17	65.25	66.33	67.42	68.52	69.63	70.75	71.88	73.01	74.16
5.7	54.88	55.89	56.90	57.92	58.95	59.99	61.04	62.09	63.16	64.23	65.32	66.41	67.51	68.62	69.74	70.87	72.01	73.16	74.32	75.48
5.8	55.85	56.87	57.90	58.94	59.98	61.04	62.11	63.18	64.27	65.36	66.46	67.58	68.70	69.83	70.97	72.12	73.28	74.44	75.62	76.81
5.9	56.81	57.85	58.90	59.95	61.02	62.09	63.18	64.27	65.37	66.49	67.61	68.74	69.88	71.03	72.19	73.36	74.54	75.73	76.92	78.13
6.0	57.77	58.83	59.89	60.97	62.05	63.14	64.25	65.36	66.48	67.61	68.76	69.91	71.07	72.24	73.42	74.60	75.80	77.01	78.23	79.46

CIRCUMFERENCE (inches)

LENGTH (inches)	13.0	13.1	13.2	13.3	13.4	13.5	13.6	13.7	13.8	13.9	14.0	14.1	14.2	14.3	14.4	14.5	14.6	14.7	14.8	14.9
3.0	40.35	40.97	41.60	42.23	42.87	43.51	44.16	44.81	45.46	46.13	46.79	47.46	48.14	48.82	49.50	50.19	50.89	51.59	52.29	53.00
3.1	41.69	42.33	42.98	43.64	44.30	44.96	45.63	46.30	46.98	47.66	48.35	49.04	49.74	50.45	51.15	51.87	52.58	53.31	54.04	54.77
3.2	43.04	43.70	44.37	45.04	45.72	46.41	47.10	47.79	48.50	49.20	49.91	50.63	51.35	52.07	52.80	53.54	54.28	55.03	55.78	56.53
3.3	44.38	45.07	45.76	46.45	47.15	47.86	48.57	49.29	50.01	50.74	51.47	52.21	52.95	53.70	54.45	55.21	55.98	56.75	57.52	58.30
3.4	45.73	46.43	47.14	47.86	48.58	49.31	50.04	50.78	51.53	52.28	53.03	53.79	54.56	55.33	56.10	56.89	57.67	58.47	59.26	60.07
3.5	47.07	47.80	48.53	49.27	50.01	50.76	51.52	52.28	53.04	53.81	54.59	55.37	56.16	56.95	57.75	58.56	59.37	60.19	61.01	61.83
3.6	48.41	49.16	49.92	50.68	51.44	52.21	52.99	53.77	54.56	55.35	56.15	56.95	57.77	58.58	59.40	60.23	61.07	61.91	62.75	63.60
3.7	49.76	50.53	51.30	52.08	52.87	53.66	54.46	55.26	56.07	56.89	57.71	58.54	59.37	60.21	61.05	61.91	62.76	63.62	64.49	65.37
3.8	51.10	51.89	52.69	53.49	54.30	55.11	55.93	56.76	57.59	58.43	59.27	60.12	60.97	61.84	62.70	63.58	64.46	65.34	66.24	67.13
3.9	52.45	53.26	54.08	54.90	55.73	56.56	57.40	58.25	59.10	59.96	60.83	61.70	62.58	63.46	64.35	65.25	66.15	67.06	67.98	68.90
4.0	53.79	54.63	55.46	56.31	57.16	58.01	58.87	59.74	60.62	61.50	62.39	63.28	64.18	65.09	66.00	66.92	67.85	68.78	69.72	70.67
4.1	55.14	55.99	56.85	57.71	58.58	59.46	60.35	61.24	62.13	63.04	63.95	64.87	65.79	66.72	67.65	68.60	69.55	70.50	71.47	72.43
4.2	56.48	57.36	58.24	59.12	60.01	60.91	61.82	62.73	63.65	64.58	65.51	66.45	67.39	68.35	69.31	70.27	71.24	72.22	73.21	74.20
4.3	57.83	58.72	59.62	60.53	61.44	62.36	63.29	64.22	65.17	66.11	67.07	68.03	69.00	69.97	70.96	71.94	72.94	73.94	74.95	75.97
4.4	59.17	60.09	61.01	61.94	62.87	63.81	64.76	65.72	66.68	67.65	68.63	69.61	70.60	71.60	72.61	73.62	74.64	75.66	76.69	77.73
4.5	60.52	61.45	62.40	63.34	64.30	65.26	66.23	67.21	68.20	69.19	70.19	71.19	72.21	73.23	74.26	75.29	76.33	77.38	78.44	79.50
4.6	61.86	62.82	63.78	64.75	65.73	66.71	67.71	68.71	69.71	70.73	71.75	72.78	73.81	74.85	75.91	76.96	78.03	79.10	80.18	81.27
4.7	63.21	64.18	65.17	66.16	67.16	68.16	69.18	70.20	71.23	72.26	73.31	74.36	75.42	76.48	77.56	78.64	79.72	80.82	81.92	83.04
4.8	64.55	65.55	66.55	67.57	68.59	69.61	70.65	71.69	72.74	73.80	74.87	75.94	77.02	78.11	79.21	80.31	81.42	82.54	83.67	84.80
4.9	65.90	66.92	67.94	68.97	70.02	71.06	72.12	73.19	74.26	75.34	76.43	77.52	78.63	79.74	80.86	81.98	83.12	84.26	85.41	86.57
5.0	67.24	68.28	69.33	70.38	71.44	72.52	73.59	74.68	75.77	76.88	77.99	79.10	80.23	81.36	82.51	83.66	84.81	85.98	87.15	88.34
5.1	68.59	69.65	70.71	71.79	72.87	73.97	75.07	76.17	77.29	78.41	79.55	80.69	81.83	82.99	84.16	85.33	86.51	87.70	88.90	90.10
5.2	69.93	71.01	72.10	73.20	74.30	75.42	76.54	77.67	78.80	79.95	81.11	82.27	83.44	84.62	85.81	87.00	88.21	89.42	90.64	91.87
5.3	71.28	72.38	73.49	74.61	75.73	76.87	78.01	79.16	80.32	81.49	82.67	83.85	85.04	86.25	87.46	88.68	89.90	91.14	92.38	93.64
5.4	72.62	73.74	74.87	76.01	77.16	78.32	79.48	80.65	81.84	83.03	84.22	85.43	86.65	87.87	89.11	90.35	91.60	92.86	94.13	95.40
5.5	73.97	75.11	76.26	77.42	78.59	79.77	80.95	82.15	83.35	84.56	85.78	87.01	88.25	89.50	90.76	92.02	93.30	94.58	95.87	97.17
5.6	75.31	76.48	77.65	78.83	80.02	81.22	82.42	83.64	84.87	86.10	87.34	88.60	89.86	91.13	92.41	93.69	94.99	96.30	97.61	98.94
5.7	76.66	77.84	79.03	80.24	81.45	82.67	83.90	85.13	86.38	87.64	88.90	90.18	91.46	92.76	94.06	95.37	96.69	98.02	99.35	100.70
5.8	78.00	79.21	80.42	81.64	82.88	84.12	85.37	86.63	87.90	89.18	90.46	91.76	93.07	94.38	95.71	97.04	98.38	99.74	101.10	102.47
5.9	79.35	80.57	81.81	83.05	84.30	85.57	86.84	88.12	89.41	90.71	92.02	93.34	94.67	96.01	97.36	98.71	100.08	101.46	102.84	104.24
6.0	80.69	81.94	83.19	84.46	85.73	87.02	88.31	89.62	90.93	92.25	93.58	94.92	96.28	97.64	99.01	100.39	101.78	103.18	104.58	106.00

LENGTH (inches)	CIRCUMFERENCE (inches)																			
	15.0	15.1	15.2	15.3	15.4	15.5	15.6	15.7	15.8	15.9	16.0	16.1	16.2	16.3	16.4	16.5	16.6	16.7	16.8	16.9
3.0	53.71	54.43	55.16	55.88	56.62	57.36	58.10	58.85	59.60	60.35	61.12	61.88	62.65	63.43	64.21	64.99	65.79	66.58	37.38	68.18
3.1	55.51	56.25	57.00	57.75	58.51	59.27	60.03	60.81	61.58	62.37	63.15	63.94	64.74	65.54	66.35	67.16	67.98	68.80	69.63	70.46
3.2	57.30	58.06	58.83	59.61	60.39	61.18	61.97	62.77	63.57	64.38	65.19	66.01	66.83	67.66	68.49	69.33	70.17	71.02	71.87	72.73
3.3	59.09	59.88	60.67	61.47	62.28	63.09	63.91	64.73	65.56	66.39	67.23	68.07	68.92	69.77	70.63	71.49	72.36	73.24	74.12	75.00
3.4	60.88	61.69	62.51	63.34	64.17	65.00	65.84	66.69	67.54	68.40	69.26	70.13	71.01	71.89	72.77	73.66	74.56	75.46	76.36	77.28
3.5	62.67	63.51	64.35	65.20	66.05	66.91	67.78	68.65	69.53	70.41	71.30	72.20	73.10	74.00	74.91	75.83	76.75	77.68	78.61	79.55
3.6	64.46	65.32	66.19	67.06	67.94	68.83	69.72	70.61	71.52	72.42	73.34	74.26	75.18	76.11	77.05	77.99	78.94	79.90	80.86	81.82
3.7	66.25	67.13	68.03	68.92	69.83	70.74	71.65	72.58	73.50	74.44	75.38	76.32	77.27	78.23	79.19	80.16	81.13	82.12	83.10	84.09
3.8	68.04	68.95	69.87	70.79	71.72	72.65	73.59	74.54	75.49	76.45	77.41	78.38	79.36	80.34	81.33	82.33	83.33	84.33	85.35	86.37
3.9	69.83	70.76	71.70	72.65	73.60	74.56	75.53	76.50	77.48	78.46	79.45	80.45	81.45	82.46	83.47	84.49	85.52	86.55	87.59	88.64
4.0	71.62	72.58	73.54	74.51	75.49	76.47	77.46	78.46	79.46	80.47	81.49	82.51	83.54	84.57	85.61	86.66	87.71	88.77	89.84	90.91
4.1	73.41	74.39	75.38	76.38	77.38	78.39	79.40	80.42	81.45	82.48	83.52	84.57	85.63	86.69	87.75	88.83	89.91	90.99	92.09	93.19
4.2	75.20	76.21	77.22	78.24	79.26	80.30	81.34	82.38	83.44	84.50	85.56	86.63	87.71	88.80	89.89	90.99	92.10	93.21	94.33	95.46
4.3	76.99	78.02	79.06	80.10	81.15	82.21	83.27	84.34	85.42	86.51	87.60	88.70	89.80	90.91	92.03	93.16	94.29	95.43	96.58	97.73
4.4	78.78	79.84	80.90	81.96	83.04	84.12	85.21	86.31	87.41	88.52	89.64	90.76	91.89	93.03	94.17	95.33	96.48	97.65	98.82	100.00
4.5	80.57	81.65	82.74	83.83	84.93	86.03	87.15	88.27	89.40	90.53	91.67	92.82	93.98	95.14	96.31	97.49	98.68	99.87	101.07	102.28
4.6	82.36	83.46	84.57	85.69	86.81	87.95	89.08	90.23	91.38	92.54	93.71	94.89	96.07	97.26	98.45	99.66	100.87	102.09	103.32	104.55
4.7	84.15	85.28	86.41	87.55	88.70	89.86	91.02	92.19	93.37	94.55	95.75	96.95	98.16	99.37	100.59	101.83	103.06	104.31	105.56	106.82
4.8	85.94	87.09	88.25	89.42	90.59	91.77	92.96	94.15	95.36	96.57	97.78	99.01	100.24	101.49	102.74	103.99	105.26	106.53	107.81	109.09
4.9	87.73	88.91	90.09	91.28	92.48	93.68	94.89	96.11	97.34	98.58	99.82	101.07	102.33	103.60	104.88	106.16	107.45	108.75	110.05	111.37
5.0	89.52	90.72	91.93	93.14	94.36	95.59	96.83	98.08	99.33	100.59	101.86	103.14	104.42	105.71	107.02	108.32	109.64	110.97	112.30	113.64
5.1	91.32	92.54	93.77	95.00	96.25	97.50	98.77	100.04	101.32	102.60	103.90	105.20	106.51	107.83	109.16	110.49	111.83	113.19	114.55	115.91
5.2	93.11	94.35	95.61	96.87	98.14	99.42	100.70	102.00	103.30	104.61	105.93	107.26	108.60	109.94	111.30	112.66	114.03	115.41	116.79	118.19
5.3	94.90	96.17	97.44	98.73	100.02	101.33	102.64	103.96	105.29	106.63	107.97	109.32	110.69	112.06	113.44	114.82	116.22	117.62	119.04	120.46
5.4	96.69	97.98	99.28	100.59	101.91	103.24	104.58	105.92	107.28	108.64	110.01	111.39	112.78	114.17	115.58	116.99	118.41	119.84	121.28	122.73
5.5	98.48	99.79	101.12	102.46	103.80	105.15	106.51	107.88	109.26	110.65	112.05	113.45	114.86	116.29	117.72	119.16	120.61	122.06	123.53	125.00
5.6	100.27	101.61	102.96	104.32	105.69	107.06	108.45	109.84	111.25	112.66	114.08	115.51	116.95	118.40	119.86	121.32	122.80	124.28	125.78	127.28
5.7	102.06	103.42	104.80	106.18	107.57	108.98	110.39	111.81	113.23	114.67	116.12	117.58	119.04	120.51	122.00	123.49	124.99	126.50	128.02	129.55
5.8	103.85	105.24	106.64	108.04	109.46	110.89	112.32	113.77	115.22	116.68	118.16	119.64	121.13	122.63	124.14	125.66	127.18	128.72	130.27	131.82
5.9	105.64	107.05	108.48	109.91	111.35	112.80	114.26	115.73	117.21	118.70	120.19	121.70	123.22	124.74	126.28	127.82	129.38	130.94	132.51	134.10
6.0	107.43	108.87	110.31	111.77	113.24	114.71	116.20	117.69	119.19	120.71	122.23	123.76	125.31	126.86	128.42	129.99	131.57	133.16	134.76	136.37

Index